BOOKTALKING ACROSS
THE CURRICULUM

BOOKTALKING ACROSS THE CURRICULUM
The Middle Years

Nancy J. Keane

2002
LIBRARIES UNLIMITED
Teacher Ideas Press
A Division of Greenwood Publishing Group, Inc.
Wes███████████████t

LIBRARIES UNLIMITED
Teacher Ideas Press
A Division of Greenwood Publishing Group, Inc.
88 Post Road West
Westport, CT 06881
1-800-225-5800
www.lu.com

ISBN 1-56308-937-8

To my children, Aureta and Alex Keane

And to the memory of my mother, Aureta C. Keane

CONTENTS

ACKNOWLEDGMENTS

I wish to thank the people who have helped with this endeavor. First, I would like to thank all the authors who gave us these marvelous stories to enjoy. With so many children's books in print, it is always difficult to limit the entries. Without these extraordinary people, this would have been a thankless task. As it was, I have spent numerous entertaining hours wrapped up in the books.

I would also like to thank the many librarians I have come in contact with. They have introduced me to books I may have missed. The library staff of the Concord (New Hampshire) School District have been very helpful, especially when I begged to borrow books from their collections. The staff of the Children's Room at Concord (New Hampshire) Public Library have also been helpful. Their fantastic collection kept me engrossed in quality literature for many, many days. They were particularly generous in retrieving books for me during their renovation when the books were not accessible to the public. My colleagues around the state have been great about suggesting books I might have missed.

The many wonderful, dedicated teachers I have had the privilege of knowing also influenced this work tremendously. Their ideas for activities and their willingness to share has helped a great deal. I have been fortunate to work with a talented group of educators.

I would also like to thank Barbara Ittner from Libraries Unlimited. She has worked with me from the start of this manuscript, offering advice and support.

Most important, I would like to thank my family. My children Aureta and Alex didn't complain too much about the amount of time I spent in the library or on the computer. They listened to the books I read to them and gave me their opinions on them. If you really want to know if a child will like a book, ask a child. If my children grew tired of my spontaneous booktalks, they didn't let on. They are the best!

INTRODUCTION

Children's literature has long been a vital part of children's lives. Stories reflect society and help children learn about their world. Children's literature also shows children different perspectives and allows them to experience events in a nonthreatening way. Historical fiction introduces them to what life was like long ago. Literary fiction introduces them to the beauty of language. Children's literature can also present valuable information and ideas about mathematics, science, and other topics. Fiction makes difficult concepts accessible because it is told in a way that is understandable to youngsters. By using children's literature to teach young learners, the teacher opens the door to expanding the exploration of topics in greater depth.

One way to excite children about reading is to use booktalks. Booktalks are short promotional presentations that tease a child into wanting to know more about specific books. Books that are not promoted often stay on the shelves to collect dust. When children hear about books, either through friends or through booktalks, they are more apt to take them down and read them.

The purpose of this book is to promote fiction reading, to show educators how books can be used to support and enhance curricular studies, and to encourage the discussion to go further into real-life activities. The emphasis is on middle school curriculum. The book is divided into chapters focusing on history, social studies, language arts and literature, mathematics, science, the arts, and physical education/sports. There is also a chapter that explores ways to use children's literature to teach critical thinking skills. The final chapter, "Just for Fun," includes humorous stories and holidays. Each chapter includes booktalks for books on that subject, as well as pertinent activity ideas, writing prompts, and/or discussion questions. A list of other books about the topic follows.

Booktalking can be a rewarding experience for both the adult and the child. Enthusiasm is infectious. The reward is connecting children to books. A booktalk is like a movie trailer. The idea is to "sell" the book. You want to give enough information to lure the audience into wanting more. A booktalk is not a review; you don't need to say whether you liked the book or not. It is assumed that you enjoyed the book and think it is worth reading because you are promoting it. You might say you found it amusing or entertaining, but you really don't need to say how you feel about the book.

These booktalks are meant to get the children interested in reading. The booktalks can easily be used by school librarians, who are often put in the position of finding support materials for the curriculum. They can also be used by public librarians making field trips to schools or speaking to groups of students about reading and books. Finally, they can be used by teachers who wish to motivate students to read and to learn. The booktalks can be modified to reflect specific needs of the population of children and your own style as a booktalker. Information given about each book includes author, title, publisher, date of publication, suggested interest level (IL—given as grade level), and suggested reading level if known (RL—given as grade level). This is followed by a booktalk that can be used as is or adapted to your own booktalking style.

In addition, activity ideas, writing prompts, and/or discussion topics are provided for each of the main booktalk titles. These are suggestions for the type of learning extensions that you and your students can make to follow up on the book's theme, and they illustrate how the books can be used to complement or enhance curricular studies. They are intended simply as starters, and there is ample opportunity for you to personalize and adapt the activities to fit your style and your students' needs.

There are also lists of additional books that can be used in conjunction with the theme of the chapter. The information given for each of these books includes author, title, publisher, date of publication, suggested interest level (IL—given as grade level), and suggested reading level if known (RL—given as grade level). For the purposes of this book, the YA designation refers to books that may be appropriate only for grades 7 or 8. A short annotation based on the Library of Congress summary statement is given with these titles.

Criteria for Book Selection

This guide covers 170 titles that appeal to middle school readers and relate to middle school curriculum. In addition, there are 330 other book suggestions. Fiction in genres ranging from mystery and fantasy to historical fiction and literary classics is included. Unless otherwise indicated, the books covered are fiction. Approximately 10 percent of the titles are nonfiction, and that is noted in the bibliographic entries.

The books chosen are all currently in print and have received positive reviews in publications specializing in children's literature. A majority of the books were published within the past 10 years. They have been selected for their age-appropriateness for middle school children. Keep in mind that books that appeal to fifth graders may be too young for eighth graders. Then again, one fifth grader may not enjoy a selection that another fifth grader adores. It is essential for you to select the material that is appropriate for and appealing to your students. Several of the selections have more mature content and styles, and I have noted those so that teachers can be especially aware that the book contains material that may be unappealing, inappropriate, or offensive to some.

Booktalks

In this guide you'll find booktalks for books that appeal to middle school students in grades 5 through 8. The booktalks are meant to entice students to read the books and learn more about the curricular subjects. They are intended as springboards, and educators should freely adapt them to reflect their style and their audiences' needs.

Interest Level

For each title, the suggested interest level (IL) is noted (as a grade level). Most of the books mentioned in this publication are designated IL 5–8. Some may be designated IL 3–6, and some are YA (young adult/high school). The IL is a guideline for letting you know what age group the book will appeal to and is meant as a guide for selection. This does not mean that only students in that grade should read the books. Some students are ready for more advanced books; some are not. These ratings are taken from professional review sources.

Reading Level

For most books, I have noted the reading level (RL). Again, this is given as a grade level and is based on levels cited in professional review sources. Reading levels are noted as grade level plus month within that level. For example, a reading level of 6.2 correlates to the second month of sixth grade. Most of the books mentioned have RLs in the middle school range, but some are lower level and some are higher. Some students want to read books at a higher interest level and an easier reading level. Some YA material does not include the RL.

Learning Extension Ideas

Extension activities are suggested for all books that have booktalks. Although these activities may be specific to the particular title, they can be easily adapted to other books with similar themes. The activities are suggestions and jumping off points for learning.

Suggested Further Reading Lists

A list of suggested readings for each of the subject categories is included, with bibliographic information and short annotations. These books have met the same criteria for selection as have the featured books.

⌘

It is hoped that teachers, school librarians, and public librarians will find inspiration in this book to use booktalking as a starting point for the discussion of themes. When children begin a lesson with enthusiasm, the lesson is sure to be a hit and the learning takes hold.

To find out more about booktalking and to access a database of ready-to-use booktalks, visit the Web page *Booktalks—Quick and Simple* at http://www.nancykeane.com. There is also a listserv to share and discuss booktalks. To join, visit *Booktalks—Quick and Simple* and click on "Join booktalkers Group" or go to http://groups.yahoo.com/group/booktalkers.

1 ❧ History and Social Studies: Introduction

> If a nation expects to be ignorant and free, in a state of civilization, it expects what never was and never will be. . . . I know of no safe repository of the ultimate powers of the society but the people themselves; and if we think them not enlightened enough to exercise their control with wholesome discretion, the remedy is not to take it from them, but to inform their discretion by education.
> —*Thomas Jefferson*

Jefferson knew that it is vital for Americans to study the history of our world and pass that knowledge on to children so that they can also share in it. Moses Mather wrote in 1775 that "the strength and spring of every free government is the virtue of the people; virtue grows on knowledge, and knowledge on education."

The study of history is not just a collection of dates and names with no connection to our lives. Unfortunately, there are some who think of the study of history as just that. Studying history helps us more than just by giving us dry facts; it helps us understand people. By examining what has happened in the past, we can understand why things are the way they are. We can see how people have benefited by their experiences, how they have reacted, and what they have learned.

History helps us understand change. By looking at the past, we are able to discern patterns and to predict future events by using these patterns. These may be economic or even weather patterns. By understanding change, we can better prepare for it. We can also put that change into context.

Studying history helps us understand our society and ourselves. We are better able to understand why things are as they are. We can look at what events shaped our world and our society. History allows us to look at our culture and put it into a larger context.

History contributes to moral understanding also. It often reveals the reasons for our mores and laws. By studying how a culture evolved and how humans interacted with each other, we are able to understand why things are as they are.

Studying history provides skills for our students, requiring the ability to assess evidence from the past. This evidence can include primary source materials as well as secondary sources and artifacts. Students are also introduced to conflicting interpretations of the same materials. The ability to assess these conflicting interpretations and make sense of them is an important skill for an educated person in our society.

Chapters 2 and 3 look at books that help in the study of history. "United States History" covers the first peoples through the later twentieth century. "World History" covers prehistory through World War II. Titles are arranged in chronological categories within these sections. For each group of titles, there are booktalks, activities to go along with the theme, and lists of further reading suggestions.

Chapter 4, on social studies, covers subjects of politics and government, which are closely related to history. Some people are fascinated by politics; some are not. No matter what their feelings are, politics affect our lives everyday. Students must have a basic understanding of how our government works and be aware of those who shape our laws. Whether it's a new education law, a local funding bill, or a dramatic international decision, we must stay informed about what is going on around us.

Social studies also deals with issues such as personal welfare and community well-being. We explore some books that deal with abuse, disabilities, gay issues, and school violence, all topics that affect our students today.

The United States is a land of immigrants. Communities are made up of people from many cultural backgrounds. Chapter 4 also investigates novels that show us what life is like in various cultures around the world. We look at immigrants trying to maintain their cultures while living in the United States. By studying what life is like in different areas of the world, students can develop a better understanding of the people of that culture. The world is becoming a much smaller community than it was before the days of television and the Internet. By understanding what life is like for people around the world, it will be easier for students to understand the many cultures found in the United States. Some culture clash is inevitable whenever diverse peoples come together, but by developing an understanding of cultural differences and similarities, this clash can be softened.

2 〰 United States History

First Peoples

Booktalk

Bruchac, Joseph. *Sacajawea: The Story of Bird Woman and the Lewis and Clark Expedition.* San Diego: Harcourt, ©2000. IL 5–8, RL 6.8

It was the Moon when the Leaves Fall from the Cottonwoods when I first saw them. We had heard that the white men were coming in boats full of many things. I ran as fast as I could to see them as they arrived. I stood on the bluff and watched. It wasn't hard to see who the important men were. They did not even look up. One was very serious looking. That was Captain Lewis. The other finally looked up and smiled. His smile had as much light as the rising sun. It was then I decided that he would be the one I would follow. And follow I did. For the next two years we traveled together. I actually did more than follow. This is my story.

Learning Extension Ideas

1. Sacajawea traveled with the explorers Meriwether Lewis and William Clark while they mapped out the West. These were important expeditions for the United States. Have the students create a map tracing the route that Sacajawea followed. Note important events along the way.

2. Working in groups, have students write plays about the life of Sacajawea. They should include at least five facts about Sacajawea and explain why she is an important historical figure. The plays can be acted out for the class.

RL = Reading Level   *IL = Interest Level*

Booktalk

Dorris, Michael. *Sees Behind Trees.* New York: Hyperion Books, 1996. IL 3–6, RL 5.2

Walnut is a young Native American boy who has a big problem. He has terrible vision. Nowadays, that is not such a big problem. You can simply go to the eye doctor and get some glasses. But Walnut is living in the 1600s and there is no eye doctor to help him. The young men of the village must prove themselves to the adults by the accuracy of their arrows. Of course, Walnut is worried that he will not become a man because of his poor eyesight. He practices and learns to rely on his other senses. He does so well during the contest that he is given the name Sees Behind Trees. Because of his ability to see the unseen, he is chosen to accompany Gray Fire in search of the mysterious land of water. But can he really see behind trees, or will he fail when all are depending on him?

Learning Extension Ideas

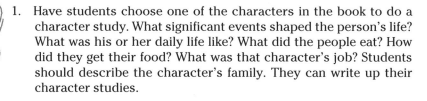

1. Have students choose one of the characters in the book to do a character study. What significant events shaped the person's life? What was his or her daily life like? What did the people eat? How did they get their food? What was that character's job? Students should describe the character's family. They can write up their character studies.

2. Have students create a timeline of the major events in the novel. Significant moments should be depicted in an illustration.

Booktalk

Erdrich, Louise. *The Birchbark House.* New York: Hyperion Books for Children, ©1999. IL 5–8, RL 5.6

"The only person left alive on the island was a baby girl." So begins the tale of Omakayas. For as long as she can remember, her family has lived on the island in Lake Superior. The Ojibwa live the way they have always lived. They follow a pattern of the seasons: Every summer they build a new birchbark house, every fall they go to ricing camp to harvest and feast, and every winter they move to the cedar log house. And they celebrate Spring with maple sugaring camp. Omakayas is happy with her life. Even though the tribe is aware of the white men who are moving ever closer to them, they feel they are safe from the outside world. Then a young stranger wanders into camp. He will change their lives forever. What does he bring with him? How will Omakayas's life change?

Learning Extension Ideas

1. Have students create a diagram showing the relationships between the characters. This can include the minor characters as well as the major ones.

2. As the European settlers required more and more land, their expansion created a problem for the Native Americans who were living in the area. The Native Americans were moved from their land and forced to move west. What happened to the Ojibwa people who once lived near Lake Superior? Have students research the time period and report on the plight of the Ojibwa or other Native Americans of the time.

Suggested Further Reading

Brown, Virginia Pounds. *Cochula's Journey.* Montgomery, Ala.: Black Belt Press, ©1996. IL 5–8, RL 4.8

This book describes the 1540 DeSoto expedition from the point of view of the daughter of an Alabama Indian chief. The marauding Spaniards devastated the village and people.

Bruchac, Joseph. *The Journal of Jesse Smoke: A Cherokee Boy.* New York: Scholastic, ©2001. IL 5–8, RL 7.9

Jesse Smoke, a 16-year-old Cherokee, begins a journal in 1837 to record stories of his people and their difficulties as they face removal along the Trail of Tears. The book includes a historical note giving details of the removal.

Durbin, William. *Wintering.* New York: Delacorte Press, ©1999. IL 5–8, RL 6.3

In 1801, 14-year-old Pierre returns to work for the North West Fur Company and makes the long and difficult journey to a winter camp. Along the way, he learns from both the other voyageurs and the Ojibwa Indians whose land they share.

Durrant, Lynda. *Echohawk.* New York: Clarion Books, ©1996. IL 5–8, RL 4.8

A 12-year-old white boy, adopted and raised by Mohicans in the Hudson River Valley during the 1730s, is sent with his younger brother to an English settlement for schooling.

Garland, Sherry. *Indio.* San Diego: Harcourt Brace, ©1995. IL 5–8, RL 5.3

Thirteen-year-old Ipa struggles to survive a brutal time of change. The Spanish begin the conquest of the native people along the Texas border.

Gates, Viola R. *Journey to Center Place.* Emeryville, Calif.: Roberts Rinehart, ©1996. IL 5–8, RL 5.5

Provides factual details about Anasazi life in A.D. 1130 through the story of three young people and their families. They are forced to leave their home because of a drought and travel the road to Center Place in what is now northwestern New Mexico.

Hobbs, Will. *Beardance.* New York: Avon Books, 1995, ©1993. IL 5–8, RL 6.1

While accompanying an elderly rancher on a trip into the San Juan Mountains, Cloyd, a Ute Indian boy, tries to help two orphaned grizzly cubs survive the winter and at the same time complete his spirit mission.

Richter, Conrad. *The Light in the Forest.* New York: Fawcett Juniper, 1991, ©1953. IL 5–8, RL 7.6

John Butler has been raised as an Indian for 11 years following his capture at the age of four. He is forcibly returned to his white parents but continues to long for the freedom of Indian life.

Shefelman, Janice Jordan. *Comanche Song.* Austin, Tex.: Eakin Press, ©2000. IL 5–8, RL 5.7

A young Comanche boy experiences his tribe's conflicts with the Tejanos in 1840s Texas.

Stainer, M. L. *The Lyon's Cub.* Circleville, N.Y.: Chicken Soup Press, ©1998. IL 5–8, RL 6.0

Jessabel is one of the survivors of the English settlement on Roanoke Island, from which everyone disappeared in 1587. Here she relates how her remaining companions live with the Croatoan Indians and try to find the missing colonists.

Colonial Times

Booktalk

Collier, James Lincoln. *The Corn Raid.* Lincolnwood, Ill.: Jamestown Publishers, ©2000. IL 5–8, RL 5.6

Meet Richard. He is 12 years old and lives in fear. You see, Richard is an indentured servant. He lives in fear that his owner will beat him or perhaps do worse. Life is not always easy in Jamestown in the early 1600s. The settlement is still young and there is much to do. One day when Richard is in the tobacco fields, he comes across a young Weyanock boy, who also becomes indentured to the brutal Mr. Layton. The two boys have much in common and become friends. When they find out that the British have plans to raid the Weyanocks' corn stores, both boys feel they should warn their people. Will their conflicting loyalties put an end to their friendship? Will the raid happen? Can the two boys resolve their differences in time?

Learning Extension Ideas

1. Have students help Richard make his decision. Encourage them to create a chart listing the pros and cons of telling Mr. Layton that the Weyanock know of the coming raid. What should Richard have done?

2. Have students research the time period. What was the relationship between the Native Americans and the colonists? Was there tension? Did the two groups live peacefully together, or was there animosity?

Booktalk

Jacobs, Paul Samuel. *James Printer: A Novel of Rebellion.* New York: Scholastic, 1997. IL YA, RL 5.6

Native American James Printer lived in Massachusetts during the late 1600s. When he was very young, he lived with the Indians. Later James was sent to live with Stephen Green, master printer, to become an apprentice and learn a trade. James was an excellent student, and as a young man his skills were almost equal those of his teacher. In 1675, James finds himself in a very precarious situation. The Indian chief, King Philip, has declared war on the English. King Philip has demanded that James return to the Indians to fight against the English. How can James take up arms against the people who raised him and against the society that he feels he belongs in? How could the once-friendly English neighbors now look at him as if he had suddenly become less than human?

Learning Extension Ideas

1. The printer was a valuable member of society during colonial times. Ask students to come up with ways the printer influenced the community. Discuss some of the ways printers contributed to everyday life in the city.

2. We have all heard the story of the first Thanksgiving. The pilgrims of Plymouth and the Native Americans had a huge feast to celebrate their new friendship. Within 50 years, the relationship between the two civilizations had deteriorated drastically. Ask students: Why? What were some of the factors that contributed to this?

3. Newspapers can serve many purposes. Have students construct a class newspaper. They can work in groups with assignments. One group can work on a story about what they are studying. Another group can concentrate on field trips. Another can create editorials, and so forth. When the newspaper is finished, have students take it home to parents.

Booktalk

Lasky, Kathryn. *A Journey to the New World: The Diary of Remember Patience Whipple.* (Dear America Series). New York: Scholastic, 1996. IL 5–8, RL 6.0

Remember Patience Whipple is a 12-year-old girl traveling with her family aboard the *Mayflower* in 1620. This is her diary. Everyone on board is excited about beginning a new life in a brand new country—especially Remember. The future looks bright, but it also holds many dangers, including two months of bad food, unfit drinking water, vicious storms, and crowded conditions. Not to mention the boredom. Is it worth it? What would it be like in America?

Learning Extension Ideas

1. The diary format is a very powerful form of story telling. It brings the characters to life and shares their inner thoughts. Have students take an historical event and write about it as if they were experiencing it firsthand. Have them write several diary entries to tell about the event and their feelings about it.

2. Have the students think about the journey across the Atlantic Ocean. Children were not allowed to take many items with them. Ask students: If you were going on a long journey and could only take one item, what would it be, and why?

Suggested Further Reading

Collier, Christopher. *Clash of Cultures: Prehistory–1638.* New York: Benchmark Books, ©1998. IL 5–8, RL 8.2

Discusses the culture of Native Americans in North America. Find out how exploration and early colonization affected them.

Cooney, Caroline B. *The Ransom of Mercy Carter.* New York: Delacorte Press, ©2001. IL 3-6, RL 5.1

In 1704, in the English settlement of Deerfield, Massachusetts, 11-year-old Mercy and her family and neighbors are captured by Mohawk Indians and their French allies. They are then forced to march through bitter cold to French Canada, where some adapt to their new lives, but others still hope to be ransomed.

Duey, Kathleen. *Sarah Anne Hartford: Massachusetts, 1651.* New York: Aladdin Paperbacks, 1996. IL 3-6, RL 4.8

Twelve-year-old Sarah breaks the Sabbath in Puritan New England. She then faces a moral dilemma when an innocent person is accused instead of her.

Forrester, Sandra. *Wheel of the Moon.* New York: Harper-Collins, 2000. IL 5–8, RL 5.9

In England in 1627, newly orphaned Pen Downing leaves her country village for London. She is then abducted and sent to Virginia, where she is made to work as an indentured servant.

Harness, Cheryl. *Three Young Pilgrims.* New York: Maxwell Macmillan International, 1992. IL 3-6, RL 5.2

Mary, Remember, and Bartholomew are among the pilgrims who survive the harsh early years in America. They live to see New Plymouth grow into a prosperous colony.

Harrah, Madge. *My Brother, My Enemy.* New York: Simon & Schuster Books for Young Readers, ©1997. IL 5–8, RL 4.8

Fourteen-year-old Robert Bradford is determined to avenge the massacre of his family. He joins with Nathaniel Bacon's rebel army in hopes of wiping out the Susquehannock Indians of Virginia.

Hermes, Patricia. *The Starving Time. Book 2: Elizabeth's Diary.* New York: Scholastic, 2001. IL 3–6, RL 4.6

Nine-year-old Elizabeth keeps a journal of her experiences in the New World as she encounters Indians, suffers hunger and the death of friends, and helps her father build their first home.

Lasky, Kathryn. *Beyond the Burning Time.* New York: Scholastic, ©1994. IL YA, RL 5.6

During the winter of 1691, accusations of witchcraft surface in a small New England village. Twelve-year-old Mary Chase fights to save her mother from execution.

Rinaldi, Ann. *The Journal of Jasper Jonathan Pierce: A Pilgrim Boy.* New York: Scholastic, 2000. IL 5–8, RL 6.1

Jasper Jonathan Pierce is a 14-year-old indentured servant traveling on the *Mayflower.* While on board, he keeps a journal of his experiences on the ship and during the building of Plymouth Plantation in 1620 and 1621.

Steins, Richard. *Colonial America.* Austin, Tex.: Raintree Steck-Vaughn, ©2000. IL 5–8, RL 6.8

This book describes daily life and important events in the American colonies during the time of British rule.

The American Revolution

Booktalk

Avi. *Fighting Ground.* New York: Harper & Row, 1984. IL 5–8, RL 5.4

Thirteen-year-old Jonathan looks forward to the war. Everyone is talking about it. His own father has been wounded in a battle. When the bells toll one April morning, Jonathan sets out to fight for America's freedom. He joins up with a group of men who are heading for battle. But no one really understands what war is all about and what they are supposed to be doing. When they encounter Hessian troops, blood is spilled. Now Jonathan begins to wonder about his decision. Will he be able to fight for a cause he believes in, or will he run away from the horror of war? What would you do?

Learning Extension Ideas

1. Jonathan's father is wounded and cannot fight. If the townspeople ask Jonathan to fight even though his father is against it, should he?

2. Ask students: What do you think the "fighting ground" is? Why?

3. Some readers think that Jonathan is a courageous young man. Ask students: Do you agree?

4. Visit Avi's Web site at http://www.avi-writer.com. Ask students: What inspired Avi to write this book?

Booktalk

Fritz, Jean. *Why Not, Lafayette?* New York: G. P. Putnam's Sons, 1999. IL 3-6, RL 5.0 (Nonfiction)

What do you want to be remembered for? As a great athlete? Maybe a famous actor? Or even a brilliant inventor? Well, as a young boy in France, Gilbert Lafayette longed for glory in battle. He hoped to find a way to be remembered. Born into a noble household, the young Marquis de Lafayette spent his days listening to stories of ancestors who had achieved glory in battle. He even had a relative who fought under Joan of Arc. But Europe in his times offered little chance for a young soldier to find glory. When young Lafayette heard of the revolution happening in America, he traveled across the ocean to join George Washington and the brave American soldiers. He soon found himself in command of a ragtag troop with few supplies. How could this group of soldiers ever hope to win a war?

Learning Extension Ideas

1. Have students learn about other important figures of the American Revolution. Ask them to think of question titles for their biographies.

2. If students were to write an autobiography about their own lives, what would be the title? Can they think of a title with a question in it?

3. Ask students: Why do you think a person from another country would get involved in a war that didn't directly affect him or her? Can you think of other examples of that happening?

Booktalk

Rinaldi, Ann. *Cast Two Shadows: The American Revolution in the South.* San Diego: Harcourt Brace, ©1998. IL 5–8, RL 7.9

Living in South Carolina in 1780, Caroline Whitaker is accustomed to the good life. Her father owns a great plantation and is very wealthy. But her life of privilege is about to end. The Revolution has come, and she cannot ignore it. She has seen her friend Kit hanged for defying the British. Her Patriot father has been arrested and sent to prison. Her brother is off fighting for the Loyalists. And now, the British have taken over the family home. Caroline becomes a prisoner in her own home, and she begins to question her beliefs. She never wanted to know about the war and the reasons behind it. Now she finds herself caught up in it. What will become of Caroline and her family? What will she learn that will change her life forever?

Learning Extension Ideas

1. When we think about the American Revolutionary War, we usually think about New England. The war did touch the southern part of the country, but much later than New England. The war was several years old before forces went to South Carolina. Have students create a timeline of battles to show when the war came to the South.

2. Ask students: Why did it take so long for the war to touch those in the South? Were Southerners involved with the war before the British arrived? In what way?

Suggested Further Reading

Collier, James Lincoln. *My Brother Sam Is Dead.* New York: Simon & Schuster Books for Young Readers, 1985, ©1974. IL 5–8, RL 5.8

This story recounts the tragedy that strikes the Meeker family during the Revolution. One son joins the rebel forces while the rest of the family tries to stay neutral in a Tory town.

Collier, James Lincoln. *War Comes to Willy Freeman.* New York: Bantam Doubleday Dell Books for Young Readers, 1987, ©1983. IL 5–8, RL 4.8

A free 13-year-old black girl in Connecticut is caught up in the horror of the Revolutionary War. She is in danger of being returned to slavery when the British kill her Patriot father and her mother disappears.

Denenberg, Barry. *The Journal of William Thomas Emerson: A Revolutionary War Patriot.* New York: Scholastic, ©1998. IL 5–8, RL 4.8

William, a 12-year-old orphan, writes about his experiences in pre-Revolutionary War Boston. He joins the cause of the Patriots, who are opposed to British rule.

Forbes, Esther. *Johnny Tremain.* Boston: Houghton Mifflin, 1971. IL 5–8, RL 5.3

After injuring his hand, a silversmith's apprentice in Boston becomes a messenger for the Sons of Liberty. Join Johnny in the days before the American Revolution.

Goodman, Joan E. *Hope's Crossing.* Boston: Houghton Mifflin, ©1998. IL 5–8, RL 5.0

Thirteen-year-old Hope is kidnapped by English Loyalists during the Revolutionary War. Now she must draw on every ounce of courage within her to respond to the ordeal.

Gregory, Kristiana. *The Winter of Red Snow: The Revolutionary War Diary of Abigail Jane Stewart.* New York: Scholastic, ©1996. IL 5–8, RL 4.8

Eleven-year-old Abigail presents a diary account of life in Valley Forge from December 1777 to July 1778. Abigail watches as General Washington prepares his troops to fight the British.

Lunn, Janet Louise Swoboda. *The Hollow Tree.* New York: Viking, 2000, ©1997. IL 5–8, RL 6.2

Fifteen-year-old Phoebe Olcott is distraught because her beloved cousin Gideon has been hanged as a British spy. Now she becomes caught up in the turmoil of war when she decides to deliver the secret message Gideon was carrying to the British general at Fort Ticonderoga.

Moore, Ruth Nulton. *Distant Thunder.* Scottdale, Pa.: Herald Press, ©1991. IL 5–8, RL 5.8

Living in the Moravian community of Bethlehem, Pennsylvania, when the American Revolution breaks out, 15-year-old Kate and her friends demonstrate how a peaceful people can help alleviate the suffering brought on by war.

Rinaldi, Ann. *Finishing Becca: A Story About Peggy Shippen and Benedict Arnold.* San Diego: Harcourt Brace, 1994. IL 5–8, RL 6.9

Fourteen-year-old Becca takes a position as a maid in a wealthy Philadelphia Quaker home. Here she witnesses the events that lead to General Benedict Arnold's betrayal of the American forces during the Revolutionary War.

Rinaldi, Ann. *A Ride into Morning: The Story of Tempe Wick.* San Diego: Harcourt Brace Jovanovich, ©1991. IL 5–8, RL 4.6

When unrest spreads at the Revolutionary War camp in Morristown, New Jersey, under the command of General Anthony Wayne, a young woman cleverly hides her horse from the mutinous soldiers who have need of it.

The Civil War

Booktalk

Beatty, Patricia. *Jayhawker.* New York: Morrow, 1991. IL 5–8, RL 6.2

Have you ever thought what your life might have been like if you lived in a different time? What if you were a teenager during the Civil War? How different your life would be from what it is now! Well, in this story, teenager Lije Tulley lives in Kansas. The year is 1861 and the Civil War has just begun. Lije is part of the abolitionist movement that helps free slaves. He rides with the Kansas Jayhawkers on several exciting raids to free slaves. Then Lije becomes a spy for the Jayhawkers. He changes his name, goes to live with a Southern family, and joins the Southern bushwhackers. Lije passes important information on to the Jayhawkers. Then he learns that the bushwhackers are planning a raid on his hometown. Now he must make a desperate choice. Should he keep his cover and continue his important work, or should he risk everything to warn the town?

Learning Extension Ideas

1. Ask students: What kind of animal is a jayhawk? Why did these men choose that name?

2. Have students select one of the minor characters from the book and write down what they know about the character: the experiences, hopes, and dreams that drive the character to act a certain

way; how that character feels about the others in the book. Then have students write a journal entry from that character's point of view.

Booktalk

Paulsen, Gary. *Soldier's Heart: A Novel of the Civil War.* New York: Delacorte Press, 1998. IL YA, RL 5.7

In 1861 in Minnesota the talk is about the coming war. The old men say there is nothing better for a man to experience than a real shooting war. The young men are swept up in the excitement and can't wait to join up. Certainly the war can't last more than a few months. Charlie Goddard is 15 years old—not old enough to join up. But he goes off to a town where he isn't known and lies about his age. Charlie finds himself enlisted in the Union Army and going off to fight the Rebs. Very quickly, Charlie discovers that war is not the glamour and glory that he heard about. First there is the endless drilling and training. Then word comes that they are moving south. During the first battle, Charlie is devastated at what he sees. Follow Charlie as he learns about life and death during the Civil War. This book is based on a real soldier who fought in the Civil War.

Learning Extension Ideas

1. There is a certain affliction that some men suffer when they return from the horrors of war. Nowadays we call it "post-traumatic stress disorder." Men returning from World War II were said to suffer from "battle fatigue." The term "shell-shocked" was used after World War I. But after the Civil War, the condition was known as "soldier's heart." Ask students: Which term do you think best describes the condition? Why?

2. Many of the conditions that soldiers endured are described in detail in this book. One of the ways Paulsen makes the conditions known to us is by describing what the soldiers have to eat and drink. Ask students: Do you think you could survive such conditions?

3. Hardtack was a staple food supply during the war. Have students make hardtack. There are many recipes available on the Internet. (One source is http://www.recipesource.com/munchies/snacks/hardtack1.html.) How would students feel if they had no other food available?

Booktalk

Rinaldi, Ann. *Mine Eyes Have Seen.* New York: Scholastic, 1998. IL YA, RL 4.1

Fourteen-year-old Annie Brown really doesn't understand how important her father is to the freedom movement, or what exactly he is doing. Then Annie and her sister-in-law set off for the Kennedy farm in Maryland to meet up with Annie's father. One of Annie's jobs is to sit on the porch and watch for anyone who may be suspicious of what her father is up to. Annie's life changed during the summer before her father leads a daring raid on Harper's Ferry. The year was 1859, and her father was the famous John Brown. This book is based on the actual journals of the real Annie Brown.

Learning Extension Ideas

1. The Civil War took place well over a hundred years ago, yet it is still a very fascinating part of American history. Ask students: Why do you think the war is so interesting to people who live today? What issues are still visible in our society?

2. Annie sees her father as just her father. At first, she has no way of knowing just how important he really is to the events in the country. Ask students: Do teenagers today really understand what their parents do? How is your life different from Annie's? How is it similar?

Suggested Further Reading

Crisp, Marty. *Private Captain: A Story of Gettysburg.* New York: Philomel Books, ©2001. IL 5–8, RL 6.5

In 1863 in Pennsylvania, 12-year-old Ben and his dog Captain set off in search of Ben's brother, who is missing from the Union Army.

Ernst, Kathleen. *Retreat from Gettysburg.* Shippensburg, Pa.: White Mane Kids, ©2000. IL 5–8, RL 7.1

In 1863, during the tense week after the Battle of Gettysburg, a Maryland boy faces difficult choices. He is forced to care for a wounded Confederate officer while trying to decide if he himself should leave his family to fight for the Union.

Hahn, Mary Downing. *Promises to the Dead.* New York: Clarion Books, ©2000. IL 5–8, RL 4.8

Twelve-year-old Jesse leaves his home on Maryland's Eastern Shore to help a young runaway slave find a safe haven during the early days of the Civil War.

Hite, Sid. *Stick and Whittle.* New York: Scholastic, 2000. IL 5–8, RL 6.1

In 1872, while journeying from Texas to Kansas, a Civil War veteran named Melvin meets a 16-year-old orphan, also named Melvin. They give each other nicknames and become partners and traveling companions on an exciting adventure.

Houston, Gloria. *Bright Freedom's Song: A Story of the Underground Railroad.* San Diego: Silver Whistle, ©1998. IL 5–8, RL 6.0

In the years before the Civil War, Bright discovers that her parents are providing a safehouse for the Underground Railroad. She helps to save a runaway slave named Marcus.

Levin, Betty. *Shadow-catcher.* New York: Greenwillow Books, ©2000. IL 5–8, RL 7.0

Although he often fancied himself a detective, Jonathan must become a real sleuth when he attempts to solve a mystery while accompanying his grandfather, a Civil War veteran and traveling photographer in Maine.

Lyons, Mary E. *Dear Ellen Bee: A Civil War Scrapbook of Two Union Spies.* New York: Atheneum Books for Young Readers, ©2000. IL 5–8, RL 5.9

A scrapbook kept by a young black girl details her experiences and those of an older white woman, "Miss Bet." Miss Bet had freed her and her family, sent her north from Richmond to get an education, and then worked to bring an end to slavery. This story is based on the life of Elizabeth Van Lew.

Matas, Carol. *The War Within: A Novel of the Civil War.* New York: Simon & Schuster Books for Young Readers, ©2001. IL YA, RL 6.0

In 1862, Union forces expel Hannah's family from Holly Springs, Mississippi, because they are Jews. Hannah reexamines her views regarding slavery and the war.

Pinkney, Andrea Davis. *Silent Thunder: A Civil War Story.* New York: Jump at the Sun/Hyperion Books for Children, ©1999. IL 5–8, RL 6.0

In 1862, 11-year-old Summer and her 13-year-old brother Rosco take turns describing how life on the quiet Virginia plantation where they are slaves is affected by the Civil War.

Wisler, G. Clifton. *Run the Blockade.* New York: HarperCollins, ©2000. IL 5–8, RL 5.6

During the Civil War, 14-year-old Henry finds adventure working as a ship's boy and lookout aboard the *Banshee*, a new British ship attempting to get past the Yankee blockade of the Southern coast.

Westward Expansion

Booktalk

Cushman, Karen. *The Ballad of Lucy Whipple.* New York: Clarion Books, 1996. IL 5–8, RL 5.0

As the miners sat around sharing conversation, one man suggested they hear a ballad. After all, he said, "there ain't nothing like a ballad on a rainy night." Lucy had never heard of a ballad, so she asked what it was. "A ballad is a poem that tells the story of the extraordinary doings of ordinary folk." This is the ballad of Lucy Whipple, born California Morning Whipple. Her mother has decided to move from their comfortable home in Massachusetts and head out West in search of gold. It had been a dream of Lucy's father before he died. Now the family is following that dream. Moving to California is the last thing Lucy wants to do, but she has no choice. The family sets up in a small mining camp named Lucky Diggings. It is not much more than a group of tents. Mama opens up a boarding tent and feeds the hungry miners. Unhappy, Lucy schemes how to return to Massachusetts. In letters written to her grandparents back home, Lucy pours out her thoughts—and her heart's desire. But what is her true heart's desire? And what does Lucy learn about it?

Learning Extension Ideas

1. In the story, Lucy's brother Butte collected 50 words for liquor. Can students name 50 words that describe an everyday item such as school? Students should work in groups. Give each group a common word. Students should come up with as many different words as they can that mean the same.

2. Using a map of the United States, trace the Whipple's journey from Massachusetts to California and eventually to the Sandwich Islands.

3. Lucy is setting up a library for the town. She has asked us to send her some books. Ask students: Which books would you send Lucy for her library? Why would those titles be appropriate?

Booktalk

Hobbs, Will. *Jason's Gold.* New York: Morrow Junior Books, 1999. IL 5–8, RL 5.1

Young Jason Hawthorne is on his way to the Klondike. He has heard that there is a huge gold strike up there, so he leaves New York City, where he is barely making enough money to live, and plans to meet up with his brothers in Seattle. He has a small inheritance there and plans to ask his brothers to finance his trip north. He knows that the journey will be hard and he will need some money to equip himself. Jason is in for a big surprise. When he gets to Seattle he finds out that his brothers have had the same idea. They have left with his money to strike it rich in the Klondike, and they have about a four-day head start. Should Jason follow them? Can he catch up? And what will he find besides adventure?

Learning Extension Ideas

1. The Gold Rush took many people to the West to search for their fortune. Some found gold, others found heartache. Compare Gold Rush fever with the twenty-first-century equivalent, the dot.com gold rush. Ask students: What are the similarities? What are the differences?

2. Many towns sprang up along the fringes of the gold territory. After the bust, many of them were abandoned and left to rot. These towns became ghost towns. Some of them have now become historical museums that show what life was like during that part of our history. Have students design an historical museum that shows what life was like during the Gold Rush. What buildings would be included? What types of artifacts would be on display?

3. Have students imagine that they are traveling to Alaska to join in the Gold Rush. Write a letter home describing their hopes and the realities. Ask students: What do you see along the way? Are you becoming discouraged, or are you still hopeful about making your fortune?

Booktalk

Murphy, Jim. *West to a Land of Plenty: Diary of Teresa Angelino Vis Cardi.* (Dear America Series). New York: Scholastic, 1998. IL 5–8, RL 4.8

Teresa Angelino Vis Cardi is an Italian immigrant traveling with her large family to the Idaho territory in the 1880s. They plan to settle in a town named Opportunity! First they travel by train through the Dakota Territory.

From there, they transfer to wagons that will take them across the rugged countryside. Along the way they face illness, Indians, and even death. You can follow the family's struggles and adventures through diary entries and find out what life was like for those traveling *West to the Land of Plenty.*

Learning Extension Ideas

1. Have students plan a trip to the West for a family living in the 1880s. What would they need for the trip? Remember that there are considerations other than what they will need for their final destination. They must eat along the way, the wagon might break down, the weather may change, and it was common for travelers to become ill.

2. Ask students: What kind of clothing would the travelers take? Why? Create a booklet that shows the variety of clothing needed by the travelers. Be sure that the clothing represents that which would be available in the 1880s.

Suggested Further Reading

Cather, Willa. *O Pioneers!* New York: Signet Classic, 1989. IL YA, RL 6.7

Alexandra, the daughter of a Swedish immigrant farmer in Nebraska, inherits the family farm and finds love with an old friend.

Conrad, Pam. *My Daniel.* New York: HarperColllins, ©1989. IL 5–8, RL 6.1

Ellie and Stevie learn about a family legacy when their grandmother tells them stories of her brother's quest for dinosaur bones on their Nebraska farm.

Conrad, Pam. *Prairie Songs.* New York: HarperCollins, ©1985. IL 5–8, RL 5.2

Louisa's life in a loving pioneer family on the Nebraska prairie is altered by the arrival of a new doctor and his beautiful but tragically frail wife.

Gregory, Kristiana. *Across the Wide and Lonesome Prairie: The Oregon Trail Diary of Hattie Campbell.* New York: Scholastic, ©1997. IL 5–8, RL 5.2

In her diary, 13-year-old Hattie chronicles her family's arduous journey from Missouri to Oregon on the Oregon Trail in 1847.

Gregory, Kristiana. *The Great Railroad Race: The Diary of Libby West.* New York: Scholastic, 1999. IL 5–8, RL 7.7

As the daughter of a newspaper reporter, 14-year-old Libby keeps a diary account of the exciting events around her during the building of the railroad in the West in 1868.

Hahn, Mary Downing. *The Gentleman Outlaw and Me—Eli: A Story of The Old West.* New York: Clarion Books, ©1996. IL 5–8, RL 4.6

In 1887, 12-year-old Eliza disguises herself as a boy and travels to Colorado. There she searches for her missing father, falls in with a gentleman outlaw, and joins him in his illegal schemes.

Holm, Jennifer L. *Our Only May Amelia.* New York: Harper-Collins, ©1999. IL 5–8, RL 6.5

While growing up in Washington state in 1899 as the only daughter in a Finnish American family of seven brothers, May Amelia Jackson resents being expected to act like a lady.

Mazzio, Joann. *Leaving Eldorado.* Boston: Houghton Mifflin, ©1993. IL YA, RL 4.8

In the late 1890s, 14-year-old Maude is abandoned by her gold-mad father in the small New Mexico Territory mining town of Eldorado. Here she struggles to survive and to hold onto her dream of becoming an artist.

Paulsen, Gary. *Mr. Tucket.* New York: Delacorte Press, 1994. IL 5–8, RL 5.5

In 1848, 14-year-old Francis Tucket is kidnapped by Pawnee Indians while on a wagon train headed for Oregon. She then falls in with a one-armed trapper who teaches her how to live in the wild.

Paulsen, Gary. *Tucket's Gold.* New York: Delacorte Press, ©1999. IL 5–8, RL 5.5

Fifteen-year-old Francis and the two children he has adopted travel across the Old West. They evade Comancheros, discover a treasure, and wind up rich beyond their wildest dreams.

Early Twentieth Century

Booktalk

Buchanan, Jane. *Gratefully Yours.* New York: Farrar, Straus & Giroux, 1997. IL 5–8, RL 5.5

When Hattie's family is killed in a tenement fire in New York, she is sent out West on an "Orphan Train" to find a new home. The Orphan Trains were set up by well-meaning people who thought that orphans from New York City would find a better home in the West where they could get plenty of sunshine and fresh air. In reality, things didn't always turn out so well. Hattie is placed with a couple in Nebraska. Henry and Elizabeth are not unkind, but they are certainly not welcoming Hattie with open arms. Henry is distant and Elizabeth is grieving over the loss of her children. Hattie feels that she is being treated more as a servant than a child. Hattie knows she should be grateful for having a place to live, but it's hard. Will Hattie ever find a way to fit in?

Learning Extension Ideas

1. Ask students: What have you learned about the Orphan Trains? What did you know before you read this book?

2. Ask students: Who were the Orphan Train riders? Who started the orphan trains? When did the orphan trains end?

3. Ask students: How did life change for the children of the Orphan Trains? Do you think the Orphan Trains were a good thing or a bad thing?

4. When the children got off the train at the stops along the way, they were inspected and asked questions about themselves. Since they wanted good homes, the children wanted to show off their best features. Have students write a short advertisement about themselves that highlights their best characteristics.

Booktalk

Curtis, Christopher Paul. *Bud, Not Buddy.* New York: Delacorte Press, 1999. IL 5–8, RL 5.6

My name is Bud, not Buddy. I don't let anyone call me Buddy. My mother named me Bud like a flower bud—not Buddy like some dog. Well, I don't tell people this, but I don't let them call me Buddy either! Mama died four years ago and I've been in and out of the children's home ever since. Once in awhile I get put in a foster home, but that never lasts for long. Times are hard right now. There's something called the Depression that's making it really hard for folks to get by. Most folks certainly don't need one more mouth to feed. When I hear I'm going to be placed into a new foster home, I know disaster is right around the corner. And I'm always right. Things get so bad at the Amos's house that I just go on the lam. My mama didn't leave me much, but she left me some papers that were really important to her. I keep them with me all the time. The papers are advertisements for a music group starring Hermann E. Calloway. He must have been really special to mama for her to keep these things. Do you want to know a secret? I think maybe this Calloway is my daddy. I'm going to start walking to Grand Rapids and look this man up. I have a feeling he's my daddy. Do you want to come along with me? Sure you do. Come on along. Just remember, it's *Bud, Not Buddy.*

Learning Extension Ideas

1. Bud had many rules for life, such as "Rules and Things Number 83: If an Adult Tells You Not to Worry, and You Weren't Worried Before, You Better Hurry Up and Start 'Cause You're Already Running Late" and "Rules and Things Number 3: If You Got to Tell a Lie, Make Sure It's Simple and Easy to Remember." Have students come up with their own "Rules and Things."

2. Bud uses a poster as a clue to finding his father. Have students create a poster that includes clues to a book they have read. Have other students try to figure out which book it is by the clues left.

3. Ask students: How much do you know about jazz? Try to find the names of five jazz bands from the 1930s.

Booktalk

Hesse, Karen. *Out of the Dust.* New York: Scholastic, 1997. IL 5–8, RL 4.5

Imagine being in the Oklahoma Panhandle in 1934 during the Great Depression. There are dust storms everywhere. The crops have failed because of drought. The wind seems to blow constantly. Dust is always in the air. Trucks, tractors, and even the pianos are lost in the dust. This is the world of 14-year-old Billie Jo, and this book tells her story. When Billie Jo's mother is killed during a terrible accident, the townspeople hold Billie Jo responsible. Even her father is no help to her. He is caught up in the despair of the Depression and turns to the bottle for solace. How will Billie Jo endure? It will take courage, you can be sure.

Learning Extension Ideas

1. Although Oklahoma was particularly hard hit by the Great Depression of the 1930s, the entire country was affected. Have students research and discuss how the Great Depression affected people in different parts of the country.

2. Billie Jo's story is told through a set of journal entries. Have students work in pairs to create journal entries about their lives. They can keep journal entries while they read the book, then their partners should respond to each entry. Entries should include thoughts about the book as well as questions they have about what they are reading or historical events mentioned. Ask students: How does this help you understand the book?

Booktalk

Lindquist, Susan Hart. *Summer Soldiers.* New York: Delacorte Press, 1999. IL 5–8, RL 6.7

Eleven-year-old Joe is happy living in California. His life revolves around his family, friends, and the sheep farm that his father runs. They are about as far away from the war in Europe as anyone would want to be—until Joe's father enlists in the army and goes off to fight in the war. Many other men in the town do the same. Joe's friend Jim lives in a different reality. His father has decided not to enlist. The kids in the town call Jim's father a coward and make fun of him and Jim. Can Joe and Jim remain friends?

Learning Extension Ideas

1. When his father enlists in the army to go fight in Europe, Joe wonders if the enlistment poster hanging in the grocery store was the reason for his father's decision. Have students create a recruitment poster that will entice young men to go off to war. What symbols will they use? What emotions should they play to?

2. Joe's father is listed as an MIA. Ask students: What's an MIA? Joe experiences a variety of emotions that are brought on by this announcement. He remembers an old tin cookie box that his father kept. Have students create their own keepsake boxes with items that may have been in a box from 1918.

3. Jim's father made a different choice about his contribution to the war effort. He chose not to go overseas to fight but to stay home and do what he could to help. Ask students: How can people contribute on the homefront during war?

Suggested Further Reading

De Young, C. Coco. *A Letter to Mrs. Roosevelt.* New York: Delacorte Press, ©1999. IL 3-6, RL 2.8

Eleven-year-old Margo fulfills a class assignment by writing a letter to Eleanor Roosevelt. She asks for help to save her family's home during the Great Depression.

Horvath, Polly. *The Happy Yellow Car.* New York: Farrar, Straus & Giroux, 1994. IL 5–8, RL 5.7

During the Depression, Gunther Grunt buys a new car with the money his wife has been saving to send their bright 12-year-old daughter to college. This sets off a chain of events that teaches the Grunts the value of their family.

Peck, Richard. *A Long Way from Chicago: A Novel in Stories.* New York: Dial Books for Young Readers, ©1998. IL 5–8, RL 4.2

A boy recounts his annual summer trips to rural Illinois with his sister during the Great Depression to visit their larger-than-life grandmother.

Porter, Tracey. *Treasures in the Dust.* New York: Joanna Cotler Books, ©1997. IL 3-6, RL 5.5

Eleven-year-old Annie and her friend Violet describe the hardships endured by their families when dust storms, drought, and the Great Depression hit rural Oklahoma.

Snyder, Zilpha Keatley. *Cat Running.* New York: Bantam Doubleday Dell Books for Young Readers, ©1994. IL 5–8, RL 5.8

Eleven-year-old Cat Kinsey builds a secret hideout to escape her unhappy home life. Here, she slowly gets to know a poor family who have come to California after losing their Texas home to the dust storms of the 1930s.

Thesman, Jean. *The Storyteller's Daughter.* Boston: Houghton Mifflin, 1997. IL 5–8, RL 5.9

Fifteen-year-old Quinn, the middle child in a Depression-era working class family, learns some secrets about her beloved father, who has always been a source of strength and optimism for his family, friends, and neighbors.

Whitmore, Arvella. *The Bread Winner.* Boston: Houghton Mifflin, 1990. IL 3–6, RL 5.2

Sarah Ann Puckett's parents are unable to find work and pay the bills during the Great Depression. Resourceful Sarah saves the family from the poorhouse by selling her prize-winning homemade bread.

Willis, Patricia. *The Barn Burner.* New York: Clarion Books, ©2000. IL 5–8, RL 5.2

In 1933, while running from a bad situation at home and suspected of having set fire to a barn, 14-year-old Ross finds comfort with a loving family that helps him make an important decision.

Wolfert, Adrienne. *Making Tracks.* New York: Silver Moon Press, 2000. IL 5–8, RL 5.5

In 1934, in the midst of the Depression, 14-year-old Harry James Harmony runs away to find his father, who has traveled to Chicago in search of work.

Yee, Paul. *Breakaway.* Toronto: Douglas & McIntyre, 2000, ©1994. IL YA, RL 4.9

Eighteen-year-old Kwok-Ken Wong works to overcome the racism that pervades 1930s Vancouver. He wins a university soccer scholarship that he hopes will take him away from the poverty of the family farm and the Chinese community to which he feels little connection.

Later Twentieth Century

Booktalk

Curtis, Christopher Paul. *The Watsons Go to Birmingham—1963: A Novel.* New York: Delacorte Press, 1995. IL 5–8, RL 5.0

The Watsons live in Flint, Michigan, where the winters are unbelievably cold. Meet 10-year-old Kenny, little sister Joetta, and older brother Byron. Kenny is a bright young man but he is always being picked on at school. Byron is now an "official juvenile delinquent." Byron's parents are afraid that all his "adventures" in Flint will get him into trouble. They decide to take him back to Birmingham, Alabama, where they were raised. Maybe a summer with Grandma Sands will straighten him out. If not, he'll just stay there come fall. What the Watsons don't realize is that the racial hatred in Birmingham is a lot stronger than when they left. In fact, hatred is so rampant that the color of your skin determines what kind of world you live in. What will life be like for the "Weird Watsons" in Birmingham? Will things change forever? Come along as *The Watsons Go to Birmingham* in 1963.

Learning Extension Ideas

1. To understand the decade of the 1960s, the students will need to know what events happened, when, and where the Watsons' story fits in. Have the students research the Civil Rights Movement and create a timeline of events that took place during that era.

2. To create an authentic atmosphere, students can listen to music (e.g., Beatles, Motown groups) and view news shows from the decade. Discuss the Ultra Glide that Mr. Watson installed in the Brown Bomber. Videotapes from the time period are available. You can show news programs, sporting events, and television shows.

Booktalk

Gaeddert, LouAnn Bigge. *Friends and Enemies.* New York: Atheneum Books for Young Readers, 2000. IL 5–8, RL 6.4

When William, the son of a Methodist minister, moves to a small Kansas town, he becomes friends with Jim, a Mennonite. When the Japanese bomb Pearl Harbor, the country goes to war. But the Mennonites are pacifists and refuse to fight in the war. This goes against the staunch patriotism that has overtaken the town. Anger and bigotry erupt, putting William and Jim in the middle. Can their friendship survive despite their differing views on the war? Can William come to understand Jim's pacifist beliefs? Can a town divided come together again?

Learning Extension Ideas

1. During World War II, Mennonites chose to serve the war effort in alternative ways rather than go against their religious beliefs. Have students research the Mennonite contributions during the war. List ways they served the country and explain how the service was valuable.

2. Have students research the Mennonites in Kansas. Ask them: Where did the Mennonites come from? Why did they leave their former home? List some of their major beliefs. Why did William have a hard time understanding Jim and his beliefs?

Booktalk

Myers, Walter Dean. *Fallen Angels.* New York: Scholastic, 1988. IL YA, RL 7.1

Richie Perry, a 17-year-old boy who lives in Harlem, dreams of going to college. It's not something that many of his peers will ever do, but Richie wants to make it. Unfortunately, his dreams are put on hold due to lack of money. Then he hears that the army will help him pay for college if he enlists and serves a tour of duty. Richie enlists in the army to get money for his family and to help him fund his education. Never in his wildest dreams does he believe he'll be sent to Vietnam. But that is exactly where he ends up. No one could ever be prepared to experience what Richie did. No one could have told him what he'd need to do to survive.

➤ **NOTE:** *Fallen Angels* depicts events that some readers may find disturbing and includes language that some may find objectionable. Be sure to preview the novel before assigning it to students.

Learning Extension Ideas

1. Find out what students already know about the Vietnam War. They can work in small groups to share what they know. Do they know anyone who served in the military in Vietnam? Have they ever heard stories of what the war was like?

2. To understand the decade of the 1960s, the students will need to know what events happened, when, and where the Vietnam War fits in. Have the students create a timeline of events that took place from 1960 to 1975. Students may want to concentrate on the war and the events related to it.

3. Use this book along with *The Watsons Go to Birmingham—1963* to teach about two of the most important struggles of the 1960s.

Booktalk

Qualey, Marsha. *Hometown.* Boston: Houghton Mifflin, 1995. IL YA

Border Baker was happy living in New Mexico until his father inherited the family home in Minnesota. Now, although he realizes that this may be a great opportunity, Border does not look forward to moving again. After all, he's already moved six times during his 16 years of life. That's all part of being a draft dodger's son. Dad insists that moving back to Minnesota will be good for both of them. It's a chance to be part of a community, a chance to put his years of moving around behind him. This was Dad's hometown. Surely they would find a welcome there. But how could Dad know what Red Cedar is like now? He hasn't been there since he left home to avoid the draft during the Vietnam War. Dad's parents had turned their backs on him and never saw him again. Now Border, named after the Canadian border that kept Dad out of the war, is paying the price for his father's decision. Everywhere he goes, he's known as the draft dodger's son. To top it off, the United States has gone to war in the Persian Gulf and a renewed feeling of patriotism is growing in the community. Can Border learn to survive in this small Minnesota town? How will Border face his own decision about war? Move back to the Bakers' *Hometown* to find out.

Learning Extension Ideas

1. Explain to students that during the Vietnam War, young men had little choice about serving in the war. The United States had a draft system in which all eligible names were included and could be chosen. Many young men chose to avoid going to war by leaving the country or filing for conscientious objector status. Those who left the country to avoid the draft were finally allowed to return years after the war was over. Men like Border's father spent years moving around this country after dodging the draft. They were not welcomed back with open arms. During the Gulf War, many of the old feelings were brought back up. Have students research the role that conscientious objectors played during the Vietnam War and how that official status was obtained. Research what life might have been like for those who left the country rather than fight in a war they didn't believe in, or for those who fought and then came home only to be shunned or forgotten.

2. Student protests were very common during the Vietnam War. Research the role that students played in the antiwar movement. Ask students: Do you feel that the student protests had an effect on the outcome of the war?

Suggested Further Reading

Davis, Ossie. *Just Like Martin.* New York: Puffin Books, 1995. IL 5–8, RL 5.9

Following the deaths of two classmates in a bomb explosion at his Alabama church, 14-year-old Stone organizes a children's march for civil rights in the autumn of 1963.

Franklin, Kristine L. *Dove Song.* Cambridge, Mass.: Candlewick Press, 1999. IL 5–8, RL 5.0

When 11-year-old Bobbie Lynn's father is reported missing in action in Vietnam, she and her 13-year-old brother must learn to cope with their own despair. They must also deal with their mother's breakdown.

Gaines, Ernest J. *The Autobiography of Miss Jane Pittman.* New York: Bantam, 1972, ©1971. IL YA, RL 8.0

A 110-year-old African-American woman reminisces about her life, which has stretched from the days of slavery to the black militancy and civil rights movements of the 1960s.

Grimes, Nikki. *Jazmin's Notebook.* New York: Dial Books, ©1998. IL YA, RL 5.8

Jazmin, an African-American teenager who lives with her older sister in a small Harlem apartment in the 1960s, finds strength in writing poetry and keeping a record of the events in her sometimes difficult life.

Holt, Kimberly Willis. *My Louisiana Sky.* New York: Henry Holt, 1998. IL 5–8, RL 5.9

Growing up in Saitter, Louisiana, in the 1950s, 12-year-old Tiger Ann struggles with her feelings about her stern but loving grandmother, her mentally slow parents, and her good friend and neighbor, Jesse.

Krisher, Trudy. *Spite Fences.* New York: Bantam Doubleday Dell Books for Young Readers, 1996, ©1994. IL YA, RL 5.7

As she struggles with her troubled relationship with her mother during the summer of 1960, a young girl is also drawn into the violence, hatred, and racial tension in her small Georgia town.

Mead, Alice. *Soldier Mom.* New York: Farrar, Straus & Giroux, 1999. IL 3–6, RL 4.0

Eleven-year-old Jasmyn gets a different perspective on life when her mother is sent to Saudi Arabia at the beginning of the Persian Gulf War. This leaves her and her baby half-brother behind in Maine in the care of her mother's boyfriend.

Nelson, Theresa. *And One For All.* New York: Bantam Double-day Dell for Young Readers, 1991, ©1989. IL 5–8, RL 6.8

Geraldine's close relationship with her older brother Wing and his friend Sam changes when Wing joins the Marines and Sam leaves for Washington to join a peace march.

Paulsen, Gary. *The Car.* San Diego: Harcourt Brace, ©1994. IL YA, RL 6.3

A teenager left on his own travels west in a kit car he built himself, and along the way picks up two Vietnam veterans, who take him on an eye-opening journey.

Qualey, Marsha. *Come in from the Cold.* Boston: Houghton Mifflin, 1994. IL YA

In 1969, the Vietnam War protest movement brings together two Minnesota teenagers.

3  World History

Prehistory

Booktalk

Howarth, Lesley. *The Pits.* Candlewick Press, 1996. IL YA

I watch as the archaeologist's daughter finds the iceman frozen in the ice. I've waited 9,000 years for someone to find him. They think he may be some kind of hero. If only they knew what a dork he really was. They have so many of the details of our life wrong. Why do they think they know what life was like for us? They can't even figure out what it is they are seeing! It's up to me to tell the real story of what life was like back in the summer of 7650 B.C. I can't believe how easy it is to use the archaeologist's computer and printer. So I, Broddy Brodson, will tell you what life was like back in the days when I was alive and living in *The Pits*.

Learning Extension Ideas

1. Ask students: How do archaeologists know things about past civilizations?

2. Ask students: How is Brod's life similar to teenage life in the twenty-first century? What are some of the problems he encounters that have a modern day equivalent? Do you think this story is realistic?

3. Have the students pretend to be archaeologists. Hand out a variety of objects (preferably not well known). These could include old tools, craft objects, kitchen supplies, and so forth. Have the students decide what another civilization may have used that object for, and explain why they think that. Students may work in pairs for this exercise.

RL = Reading Level   *IL = Interest Level*

Booktalk

Denzel, Justin. *Boy of the Painted Cave.* New York: Philomel Books, ©1988. IL 3–6, RL 5.8

Tao has lived 14 summers, but he shouldn't have lived even one. Born with a deformed foot, his destiny was to be left for the animals to kill. After all, life among the clan is not easy, and there is no place for a boy with a deformed foot. How could he ever become a valuable member of the society? He has learned to hunt and contribute to the food supply of the clan. He is not like the others his age, though. His one passion is painting. Whenever he gets the opportunity, he draws animal shapes in the sand. He must be very careful about doing this because it is forbidden for anyone other than the shaman to paint the animals. One day, the great Shaman himself finds Tao's paintings. Now what will become of Tao? Will he be banished? Will he be sent to be devoured by the wild animals?

Learning Extension Ideas

1. Ask students: Why do you think it was forbidden for anyone other than Graybeard to paint in the caves? Name at least five animals that Tao painted. What were some of the materials used to create the paintings?

2. Have students try to replicate the techniques used to create the cave paintings. They can use sticks and feathers as drawing tools. Have them create their own animal drawings. This can be done on a large classroom mural or on individual papers. Use classroom paint supplies.

Booktalk

Lasky, Kathryn; illustrated by Rocco Baviera. *First Painter.* New York: Dorling Kindersley, 2000. IL 3–6, RL 4.1

After the death of her mother, young Mishoo must take her place as the tribe's Dream Catcher. Mishoo lives in a long ago time—a time of cave people. Mishoo's people are slowly dying because of a long drought. Now it is up to Mishoo to bring the rain. Mishoo must catch the dream that will bring the much-needed rain that can save her people. One night she dreams of her mother, who tells her to go to the cave of the she-tiger. Mishoo is afraid but knows she must follow her vision and go. What awaits Mishoo in the cave? What must she do to bring the rain? Will it work?

Learning Extension Ideas

1. In this book, Lasky has portrayed Mishoo as the first person to paint in a cave. Of, course, we don't know who was first or even when cave painting began. Ask students: Why do you suppose cave painting began? Why was most prehistoric art about animals and hunting? Why is it important to preserve examples of prehistoric art?

2. The cave painting was done in the form of pictographs. Have students study pictures of some examples and discuss what they might say. Ask students: What do the symbols mean to us?

Suggested Further Reading

Brooke, William J. *A Is for Aarrgh!* New York: J. Cotler Books, ©1999. IL 5–8, RL 6.0

Mog, a young boy living during the Stone Age, discovers words and language. He teaches his fellow cave dwellers how to talk, thus altering the course of history.

Cowley, Marjorie. *Anooka's Answer.* New York: Clarion Books, ©1998. IL 5–8, RL 6.6

While living in a river valley in southern France during the Upper Paleolithic era, 13-year-old Anooka rejects the ways of her clan. She sets out to make another kind of life for herself.

Cowley, Marjorie. *Dar and the Spear-Thrower.* New York: Clarion Books, ©1994. IL 5–8, RL 5.7

A young Cro-Magnon boy living 15,000 years ago in southeastern France is initiated into manhood by his clan. He then sets off on a journey to trade his valuable fire rocks for an ivory spear thrower.

Craig, Ruth. *Malu's Wolf.* New York: Orchard Books, ©1995. IL 3–6, RL 4.8

Malu is permitted to raise a wolf pup, which eventually is instrumental in bringing about significant changes in the lives and traditions of the young girl's Stone Age clan.

Dickinson, Peter. *A Bone from a Dry Sea.* New York: Bantam Doubleday Dell Books for Young Readers, ©1992. IL YA, RL 6.8

In two parallel stories, an intelligent female member of a prehistoric tribe becomes instrumental in advancing the lot of her people, and the daughter of a paleontologist is visiting him on a dig in Africa when important fossil remains are discovered.

Dickinson, Peter. *Mana's Story.* New York: Grosset & Dunlap, ©1999. IL 5–8, RL 7.0

Mana and the other Kin, a band of people living in prehistoric times, search for food on the edge of a great marsh. There they fight a new enemy, the dangerous killers whom they name the demon men.

Dickinson, Peter. *Noli's Story.* New York: Grosset & Dunlap, ©1998. IL 5–8, RL 4.6

About 200,000 years ago, after she and Suth rescue four small children following an attack on Good Place, Noli heeds the warnings of Moonhawk and leads the group to safety.

Dickinson, Peter. *Po's Story.* New York: Putnam & Grosset, ©1998. IL 5–8, RL 6.9

As a member of the Kin, a band of people living in prehistoric times, young Po wants to prove his bravery but finds that doing so requires overcoming great obstacles.

Dickinson, Peter. *Suth's Story.* New York: Putnam & Grosset, ©1998. IL 5–8, RL 4.2

When cut off from their Kin and lost in the desert 200,000 years ago, Suth and five other orphans struggle to survive and to find their way to safety.

Turnbull, Ann. *Maroo of the Winter Caves.* New York: Clarion Books, ©1984. IL 3–6, RL 5.1

Maroo is a girl living in the late Ice Age. She must take charge after her father is killed and lead her little brother, mother, and aged grandmother to the safety of the winter camp before the first blizzards strike.

Ancient Civilizations

Booktalk

Scieszka, Jon. *See You Later, Gladiator.* New York: Viking, 2000. IL 3–6, RL 4.8

Joe, Sam, and Fred are friends who have shared many adventures. They are the Time Warp Trio, and they possess a magic book that allows them to time travel to anywhere they want. This time, the time travel is just an accident. The boys are wrestling around when Fred accidentally bumps into the bookcase and makes contact with the Book. The boys aren't aware of this until they find themselves facing a gladiator in ancient Rome! How can three young boys hope to compete with a well-trained gladiator? Come with the Trio as they attend gladiator school and learn about life in ancient Rome.

Learning Extension Ideas

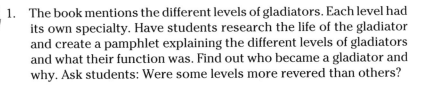

1. The book mentions the different levels of gladiators. Each level had its own specialty. Have students research the life of the gladiator and create a pamphlet explaining the different levels of gladiators and what their function was. Find out who became a gladiator and why. Ask students: Were some levels more revered than others?

2. Ask students: How does the life of a gladiator in ancient Rome compare to that of a professional athlete today (e.g., a football player or a professional wrestler)? How do the audiences treat them? What is their social status? Present your findings.

Booktalk

Snyder, Zilpha Keatley. *Egypt Game.* New York: Atheneum Books for Young Readers, ©1976. IL 3–6, RL 6.6

Meet April Hall, a lonely, insecure 11-year-old who has come to live with her grandmother. When she first meets the new girl in school, Melanie Ross, the two girls assume they have nothing in common and they don't expect to become friends. Well, that all changes when they discover that they are both wild about ancient Egypt! April and Melanie love everything about Egypt. The two quickly become best friends. They discover a secret place behind a vacant lot that they call Egypt. There they create different "Egyptian" games. They perform ceremonies, offerings, and even sacrifices. And then things begin getting weird.

Learning Extension Ideas

1. Have students learn the meanings of the names and symbols used in the book. Use a hieroglyphics dictionary or Web site to decipher them. A good source of information about hieroglyphics is http://www.virtual-egypt.com/newhtml/hieroglyphics. Have students discuss the use of symbols to represent letters in the dictionary. Have them create a symbol to represent themselves.

2. In the book, the children created ceremonies. Have the students analyze and describe one of the ceremonies. Then they can work in groups to create their own; instruct them to be as creative as they can.

Booktalk

Wilson, Diane Lee. ***To Ride the Gods' Own Stallion.*** **New York: Dorling Kindersley, 2000. IL YA, RL 6.1**

It would have been better if you had never been born. How could a father possibly say that about his own son? But those are the exact words that Soulai heard from his father. His father has so little regard for Soulai that he sells his son into slavery to pay off a debt. Soulai is a 13-year-old boy living near Nineveh, the main city in the ancient kingdom of Assyria. The year is 640 B.C. Soulai is marched to Nineveh, where he is sold again, this time to the King's son, Prince Habasle, a spoiled, cruel boy who is about Soulai's age. Soulai is assigned to work in the king's stables taking care of the horses. There he finds Ti, a magnificent stallion that has the gods' markings on his shoulder. It is said that this horse will lead the soldiers into victory. Soulai comes to love this horse and can't stand the thought of the cruel prince leading this horse to his death in battle. Then, through a series of unexpected events, Soulai and Ti become forever intertwined.

Learning Extension Ideas

1. Throughout the book, there are many examples of stories being used to relate history or to tell a moral. Have the students create a story to depict an event in the news. The story should have a moral. An example is a story of an unfortunate event caused by teenaged smoking. The moral would be that teens should not smoke.

2. Ask students: Were the characters mentioned in this book based on real people? Have the students research the events and time period to find out. Did the Library of Ashurbanipal really exist? If so, does it still exist today?

Suggested Further Reading

Blacklock, Dyan. *Pankration: The Ultimate Game.* Morton Grove, Ill.: A. Whitman, 1999. IL 5–8, RL 4.5

Having been kidnapped from a ship leaving plague-ridden Athens in 430 B.C., 12-year-old Nic attempts to escape his captors and keep his promise to meet his friend at the Olympic games.

Bunting, Eve. *I Am the Mummy Heb-Nefert.* San Diego: Harcourt Brace, ©1997. IL 3–6, RL 4.2

A mummy recalls her past life in ancient Egypt as the beautiful wife of the pharaoh's brother.

Carter, Dorothy Sharp. *His Majesty, Queen Hatshepsut.* New York: J. B. Lippincott, ©1987. IL 5–8, RL 6.4

A fictionalized account of the life of Hatshepsut, a queen in ancient Egypt who declared herself king and ruled as such for more than 20 years.

Fletcher, Susan. *Shadow Spinner.* New York: Atheneum Books for Young Readers, ©1998. IL 5–8, RL 5.5

When Marjan, a 13-year-old crippled girl, joins the sultan's harem in ancient Persia, she gathers for Shahrazad the stories that will save the queen's life.

Galloway, Priscilla. *Aleta and the Queen: A Tale of Ancient Greece.* Toronto: Annick Press, ©1995. IL 3–6, RL 6.2

When her husband Odysseus leaves to fight at Troy, Queen Penelope is left to rule Ithaca for 19 years.

Gormley, Beatrice. *Miriam.* Grand Rapids, Mich.: Eerdmans Books for Young Readers, 1999. IL 5–8, RL 6.0

While living in the pharoah's palace in ancient Egypt, Miriam, the sister of Moses in the Hebrew scriptures, struggles to remain loyal to her people and her God.

Lester, Julius. *Pharaoh's Daughter: A Novel of Ancient Egypt.* San Diego: Silver Whistle/Harcourt, 2000. IL YA, RL 5.0

A fictionalized account of a biblical story in which an Egyptian princess rescues a Hebrew infant who eventually becomes a prophet of his people. In the meantime, his sister finds her true self as a priestess to the Egyptian gods.

Macaulay, David. *Rome Antics.* Boston: Houghton Mifflin, 1997. IL 3–6, RL 5.5

A pigeon carrying an important message takes readers on a unique tour, which includes both ancient and modern parts of the city of Rome.

Rosenthal, Paul. *Yo, Aesop!: Get A Load of These Fables.* New York: Simon & Schuster Books for Young Readers, ©1998. IL 3–6, RL 5.5

Contains nine modern stories written to illustrate the lessons introduced by Aesop in his ancient Greek fables.

Speare, Elizabeth George. *The Bronze Bow.* Boston: Houghton Mifflin, ©1989. IL 5–8, RL 6.5

A young boy seeks revenge against the Romans for killing his parents but is turned away from vengeance by Jesus.

Middle Ages

Booktalk

Cooper, Susan. *King of Shadows.* New York: Margaret K. McElderry Books, 1999. IL 5–8, RL 7.0

Nat Field has the chance of a lifetime. An aspiring actor, he is chosen to join a prestigious troupe of actors who will be traveling to London to perform one of Shakespeare's plays in the Globe Theatre. This is an amazing adventure for anyone, but especially for a young boy from South Carolina. Then, after arriving in London, he begins to feel a bit giddy. Nat feels like the world is spinning, and he becomes very ill. He wakes to find himself surrounded by people he doesn't know in a world totally unfamiliar to him. To his surprise, he realizes that he is now living in London in the year 1599! But remember, the play must go on!

Learning Extension Ideas

1. Life in Elizabethan London is described in detail in this book. Have the students write about what is similar to and what is different from their world today.

2. Ask students: If you could time travel to any place or time in the world, where would you travel? Why?

Booktalk

Sturtevant, Katherine. *At the Sign of the Star.* New York: Farrar, Straus & Giroux, 2000. IL 5–8, RL 6.3

Meg Moore is a happy 12-year-old living in seventeenth-century London. Although her mother has passed away, she has a good life living with her father, who is a successful bookseller. Meg loves helping her father out in the shop. She has the chance to read all the wonderful books. She also gets to meet the famous authors. She enjoys talking with the customers about the latest books. She knows where her life is heading. She will inherit her father's business and his copyrights, marry a bookseller, and work side by side with him in the shop. Then one night Meg sees a comet in the sky. Everyone knows that a comet foretells a tragedy. But Meg has no idea how her life is about to change. In fact, all her dreams are to be dashed. Her father is going to remarry, and that means that Meg will no longer be his heir. When her stepmother begins to train Meg to be a house servant, Meg just can't come to terms with her new life. What can she do? Will things work out? Will her father send her away so he can start a new life?

Learning Extension Ideas

1. Have students compare Meg's life in seventeenth-century London to what her life would be like today. Ask students: How would her life be different? What would be her options now?

2. In the book, Meg is being trained to be a servant. Have the students research some of the occupations that were common for women during that era. Ask students: What jobs were strictly forbidden for women?

Booktalk

Temple, Frances. *The Ramsay Scallop.* New York: Orchard Books, 1994. IL YA, RL 5.6

Elenor and Thomas are betrothed, but 14-year-old Elenor is not happy about her upcoming marriage. She barely knows Thomas and doesn't really like him all that much. Thomas has just returned from the Crusades and he isn't ready to marry. But the year is 1299 and young people must do what they are told. Now Father Gregory will send Elenor and Thomas on a pilgrimage to Spain. What will happen to them on their journey?

Learning Extension Ideas

1. In the book, Etienne tells the story of Roland. Afterwards, there is a discussion about heroes. The women note that men may be heroes for what they do. Women may be heroes for what they think or what happens to them. Ask students: How do you feel about these conclusions? Come up with examples to support your opinions.

2. Ask students: What does the title refer to? What is a scallop, and why is it significant in this story?

3. In the book, Thomas has just returned from the Crusades. Have the students research the Crusades and then write about what Thomas's life was like while fighting in the wars.

Suggested Further Reading

Blackwood, Gary L. *Shakespeare's Scribe.* New York: Dutton Children's Books, ©2000. IL 3–6, RL 6.0

In plague-ridden England in 1602, a 15-year-old orphan boy, who has become an apprentice actor, goes on the road with Shakespeare's troupe and finds out more about his parents along the way.

Cohen, Barbara. *Canterbury Tales.* New York: Lothrop, Lee & Shepard, ©1988. IL 5–8, RL 5.2

A prose retelling of four tales from Chaucer's *Canterbury Tales,* in which travelers on a pilgrimage to Canterbury in the Middle Ages share their stories.

De Angeli, Marguerite. *The Door in the Wall.* New York: Doubleday, 1989, ©1949. IL 3–6, RL 6.5

A crippled boy in fourteenth-century England proves his courage and earns recognition from the king.

Graham, Harriet. *A Boy and His Bear.* New York: Margaret K. McElderry Books, 1996. IL 3–6, RL 5.2

Dickon rescues a bear cub friend from certain death at the hands of bear baiters in Elizabethan England. Told in part from the point of view of the cub.

Levitin, Sonia. *The Cure.* San Diego: Silver Whistle/Harcourt Brace, ©1999. IL YA, RL 4.7

A young boy living in 2407 collides with the past when he finds himself in the town of Strasbourg in 1348. Here he confronts the anti-Semitism that sweeps through Europe during the Black Plague.

Morris, Gerald. *Parsifal's Page.* Boston: Houghton Mifflin, 2001. IL 5–8, RL 6.0

In medieval England, 11-year-old Piers's dream comes true when he becomes page to Parsifal, a peasant whose quest for knighthood reveals important secrets about both of their families.

Platt, Richard. *Castle Diary: The Journal of Tobias Burgess, Page.* Cambridge, Mass.: Candlewick Press, 1999. IL 5–8, RL 6.2

As a page in his uncle's castle in thirteenth-century England, 11-year-old Tobias records his experiences learning how to hunt, play games of skill, and behave in noble society. Includes notes on noblemen, castles, and feudalism.

Springer, Nancy. *Rowan Hood, Outlaw Girl of Sherwood Forest.* New York: Philomel Books, ©2001. IL 5–8, RL 7.1

In her quest to connect with Robin Hood, the father she has never met, 13-year-old Rosemary disguises herself as a boy and befriends a half-wolf, half-dog, a runaway princess, and an overgrown boy whose singing is hypnotic. She also makes peace with her elfin heritage.

Vining, Elizabeth Gray. *Adam of the Road.* New York: Viking, ©1970, ©1942. IL 5–8, RL 6.1

The adventures of an 11-year-old boy in thirteenth-century England as he searches for his father and his dog.

Williams, Laura E. *The Executioner's Daughter.* New York: Henry Holt, 2000. IL 5–8, RL 7.5

In fifteenth-century Europe, 13-year-old Lily, daughter of the town's executioner, decides whether to fight against her destiny and rise above her fate.

World War I

Booktalk

Brewster, Hugh. *Anastasia's Album.* New York: Hyperion Books, 1996. IL 5–8, RL 5.9 (Nonfiction)

Anastasia was a princess. She was the daughter of Nicholas II, who was czar of Russia in the early 1900s. She lived the life of royalty until she mysteriously disappeared in 1918. Did her father's enemies kill her? Did she escape to another country? Throughout the years, several women have claimed to be the missing princess but, for more than 80 years, the story of Anastasia remained a mystery. Here is the true story of Grand Duchess Anastasia, told through actual photographs and journal entries. The epilogue of the book tells the story surrounding the mystery of Anastasia's disappearance in 1918. To learn what really happened to the little princess, read *Anastasia's Album.*

Learning Extension Ideas

1. Ask students: What was Russia's involvement in World War I? Who were their allies? Why was Anastasia's family executed? Who succeeded them?

2. Ask students: If Anastasia were still alive today, what do you think she would be doing? Have students write a short narrative that describes what they think Anastasia's life would be like now.

Booktalk

Lawrence, Iain. *Lord of the Nutcracker Men.* New York: Delacorte Press, ©2001. IL 5–8, RL 5.2

Do you have a favorite toy that you like to play with? Well, Johnny sure does. He loves to play with his toy nutcracker soldiers. His father has made them for him, and they are very special. Johnny plays war with nutcracker soldiers even though he doesn't really understand what war is. The war in Europe seems so far away. It's 1914, and soon bombs begin to fall on London. Johnny's father enlists in the army. Johnny is sent to live with his aunt in the country to stay safe from the bombs. He is very unhappy living in the country and misses his family. With each letter his father sends to Johnny comes another toy soldier, each one depicting someone his father has met in the war. As Johnny plays war with his soldiers, he begins to believe that what happens in the garden dictates what is happening in the war. Could it possibly be true? And what of Johnny's father? What will happen to him when his soldier breaks?

Learning Extension Ideas

1. Have students research what life was like for those living in London during the bombings. Ask students: Were the people warned of the coming bombs? What did they do while the bombs were falling? Did many people leave London during that time? How long did the bombing campaign last?

2. When the Germans first began the bombing runs on London, they used zeppelins. Have the students research zeppelins. Ask them: What were they? How did they work? Why were they discontinued?

Booktalk

Rostkowski, Margaret I. *After the Dancing Days.* New York: Harper & Row, 1988. IL 5–8, RL 5.8

Has someone important to you ever gone away for a long time? Maybe on a business trip or on a vacation? How did you feel when he or she returned? Were you happy, or angry with that person for having left you? Annie is really excited and happy that her father is coming home. Her father is finally returning from the war. It seems as if he has been gone forever. As they wait for her father to come off the train, Annie sees that many of the soldiers are horribly disfigured. At first, she turns away because she just cannot bear to see the men who have suffered so much. Later, she gathers her courage and goes with her grandfather to the hospital where her father works. She sits with him as he reads to a family friend who was injured in the war. Follow Annie as she comes to terms with the huge toll that war takes and as she and her family try to put the pieces back together *After the Dancing Days*.

Learning Extension Ideas

1. At the end of the war, newspapers carried many stories about the heroic deeds of returning soldiers. Have students write up an editorial that may have appeared during that time describing a soldier trying to put his life back together after experiencing war.

2. Ask students: What holiday was declared at the end of the war? Is it still celebrated today? How should we honor the people who fought in wars to ensure our freedom? Have students write a thank-you note to a fictitious or real soldier in appreciation of acts of valor.

Suggested Further Reading

Hahn, Mary Downing. *Anna All Year Round.* New York: Clarion Books, ©1999. IL 3–6, RL 4.1

Eight-year-old Anna experiences a series of episodes, some funny, others sad. They each involve friends and family during a year in Baltimore just before World War I.

Helprin, Mark. *A Soldier of the Great War.* San Diego: Harcourt Brace, ©1991. IL YA

Alessandro Giuliani tells his young companion the story of his life: how he became a soldier, a hero, a prisoner, and a deserter during World War I.

Kinsey-Warnock, Natalie. *The Night the Bells Rang.* New York: Puffin Books, 2000, 1991. IL 3–6, RL 5.6

The last year of World War I is an eventful one for Vermont farm boy Mason as he helps with the chores, tries to get along with his little brother, and sees an older bully go off to the war.

McKay, Sharon. *Charlie Wilcox.* Toronto: Stoddart Kids, 2000. IL 5–8, RL 5.4

Charlie Wilcox sets out to prove that he can follow the family tradition and go to sea in spite of his small size and clubfoot. But he finds himself headed for war instead.

Meyer, Carolyn. *Anastasia, the Last Grand Duchess.* New York: Scholastic, 2000. IL 5–8, RL 5.0

A novel in diary form in which the youngest daughter of Czar Nicholas II describes the privileged life her family led up until the time of World War I. She also describes the tragic events that befell them.

Myers, Anna. *Fire in the Hills.* New York: Walker, 1996. IL 5–8, RL 5.5

After her mother's death, 16-year-old Hallie faces changes in her life in the hills of eastern Oklahoma in 1918, as she takes over caring for her family and begins thinking about life as a woman.

Phillips, Michael R. *Wayward Winds.* Minneapolis, Minn.: Bethany House, ©1999. IL YA, RL 7.1

Twenty-year-old Amanda Rutherford, having fled the family estate, is determined to make an impact and prove her independence in pre-World War I London.

Schur, Maxine. *Sacred Shadows.* New York: Dial Books, ©1997. IL 5–8, RL 5.9

When her German hometown becomes part of Poland after World War I, Lena, a young German Jew, struggles to come to terms with the anti-Semitism and anti-German hatred that seem to be growing around her.

Seredy, Kate. *The Singing Tree.* New York: Puffin Books, 1990. IL 3–6, RL 5.5

Life changes drastically for a Hungarian family when World War I upsets their peaceful, contented existence and the children are left in charge of the farm.

Skurzynski, Gloria. *Goodbye, Billy Radish.* New York: Aladdin Paperbacks, 1996. IL 5–8, RL 5.9

In 1917, as the United States enters World War I, 10-year-old Hank sees change all around him in his western Pennsylvania steel mill town and feels his older Ukrainian friend Billy drifting away from him.

World War II

Booktalk

Isaacs, Anne. *Torn Thread.* New York: Scholastic, ©2000. IL 5–8, RL 6.8

Eva is not especially happy living in the ghetto with her father and her sister Rachel, but at least they're together. Polish Jews have been forced from their homes. Eva's family must share a small room in the ghetto with other families. Things get worse when German soldiers take Rachel away. Eva and her father hope every day that she will be returned. When Rachel is located in a labor camp in Czechoslovakia, arrangements are made for Eva to join her. Eva begs her father to let her stay in the ghetto with him, but she is told she will be safe in the labor camp—she will be with her sister. What awaits Eva as she is sent to Parschnitz? Will the girls survive their time in the camp? Does her father's difficult decision save Eva's life?

Learning Extension Ideas

1. Have students create a map showing Eva's long journey. Ask them: What are some of the things she might have seen along the way? What about her long walk to the factory? What would she have encountered on her trek?

2. This story is based on the real-life story of Eva Buchbinder. Ask students what questions they would have for her if they were able to meet her.

Booktalk

Lowry, Lois. *Number the Stars.* New York: Dell, 1990. IL 5–8, RL 4.9

Annemarie and Ellen are best friends. They have been living fairly normal lives in Copenhagen during World War II, but there is one major difference between the girls: Ellen is Jewish. When word reaches Ellen's parents that the Germans plan to arrest the Jews in the city, they decide to leave before it's too late. On the eve of Jewish New Year, most of the Jewish people, including Ellen's parents, flee the city. It is arranged that Ellen will stay with Annemarie's family in the city to keep her safe. When the German soldiers raid the home, the family convinces them that Ellen is their daughter Lise. Will this work? Will Ellen be safe? To find out about the Danish Resistance during World War II, read *Number the Stars*.

Learning Extension Ideas

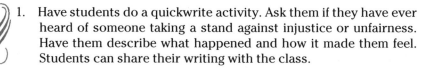

1. Have students do a quickwrite activity. Ask them if they have ever heard of someone taking a stand against injustice or unfairness. Have them describe what happened and how it made them feel. Students can share their writing with the class.

2. Lise and Peter were courageous characters. Have the students create a memorial to these characters. They can draw pictures, create newspaper clippings, write testimonials, and so forth. Information should be drawn from the story.

3. One of the major themes of this book is bravery. We are shown ordinary citizens who exhibit courage beyond what can be expected of them. Have students write about what bravery means to them. Ask them: Can brave people experience fear? Discuss what separates brave people from others.

Booktalk

Tunnell, Michael O. *Brothers in Valor: A Story of Resistance.* New York: Holiday House, ©2001. IL 5–8, RL 8.7

What would you do? It's hard to answer that question until you are put in a situation that tests you. Three Mormon teenagers must answer that question when they find themselves living under Hitler's rule in 1937. At first, Rudi, Helmuth, and Karl decide to go along and do things they don't believe in so their parents will not be hurt. They join the Nazi Youth movement even though they don't believe in the teachings. But then they realize that they just can't sit back and do nothing. They must find a way to fight back. They decide they must do something. But what can three young boys do? How can they possibly fight against the entire Nazi regime? Find out how the boys answer the question, "What would you do?"

Learning Extension Ideas

1. Ask students: Why was it so difficult to organize resistance during the Nazi occupation? Why were bullies so dominant in Nazi Youth groups? What is the importance of learning about rescuers and resistors? Why is so little known about resistance groups in Germany?

2. The Nazis believed that children should be taught to believe in their movement from a very young age. History books were rewritten to show the superiority of Germany. Science books were rewritten to prove that the Aryan race was superior. Have students research the Nazi Youth movement and list ways the government tried to influence children.

Suggested Further Reading

Booth, Martin. *War Dog: A Novel.* New York: Margaret K. McElderry Books, 1997. IL YA, RL 5.7

After her owner is arrested for poaching, the dog Jet is requisitioned by the British Army and sees duty on the beach at Dunkirk. Here she searches for survivors of Germany's bombing raids on English cities, and she works in Italy at the end of the war.

Denenberg, Barry. *The Journal of Ben Uchida, Citizen 13559: Mirror Lake Internment Camp.* New York: Scholastic, 1999. IL 5–8, RL 6.2

Twelve-year-old Ben Uchida keeps a journal of his experiences as a prisoner in a Japanese internment camp in Mirror Lake, California, during World War II.

Drucker, Malka. *Jacob's Rescue: A Holocaust Story.* New York: Bantam Doubleday Dell Books for Young Readers, 1994, ©1993. IL 5–8, RL 5.3

In answer to his daughter's questions, a man recalls the terrifying years of his childhood, when a brave Polish couple, Alex and Mela Roslan, hid him and other Jewish children from the Nazis. Based on a true story.

Levitin, Sonia. *Journey to America.* New York: Atheneum Books for Young Readers, 1993, ©1970. IL 5–8, RL 5.7

A Jewish family fleeing Nazi Germany in 1938 endures innumerable separations before they are once again united.

Matas, Carol. *In My Enemy's House.* New York: Simon & Schuster Books for Young Readers, ©1999. IL YA, RL 4.5

When German soldiers arrive in Zloczow during World War II, a young Jewish girl must decide whether to conceal her identity and work for a German Nazi in order to survive.

Mazer, Harry. *A Boy at War: A Novel of Pearl Harbor.* New York: Simon & Schuster Books for Young Readers, ©2001. IL 5–8, RL 8.5

While fishing with his friends off Honolulu on December 7, 1941, teenaged Adam is caught in the midst of the Japanese attack. Through the chaos of the subsequent days, he tries to find his father, a naval officer who was serving on the U.S.S. *Arizona* when the bombs fell.

Mazer, Norma Fox. *Good Night, Maman.* San Diego: Harcourt Brace, ©1999. IL 5–8, RL 5.0

After spending years fleeing from the Nazis in war-torn Europe, 12-year-old Karin Levi and her older brother Marc find a new home in a refugee camp in Oswego, New York.

Napoli, Donna Jo. *Stones in Water.* New York: Dutton Children's Books, 1997. IL 5–8, RL 6.5

After being taken by German soldiers from a local movie theater along with other Italian boys, Roberto is forced to work in Germany. He then escapes into Ukraine in winter, before desperately trying to make his way back home to Venice.

Nolan, Han. *If I Should Die Before I Wake.* San Diego: Harcourt Brace, ©1994. IL YA, RL 4.9

As Hilary, a neo-Nazi initiate, lies in a coma, she is transported back to Poland at the onset of World War II into the life of a Jewish teenager.

Watkins, Yoko Kawashima. *So Far from the Bamboo Grove.* New York: Beech Tree Books, 1994, ©1986. IL 5–8, RL 6.0

A fictionalized autobiography, in which 11-year-old Yoko escapes from Korea to Japan with her mother and sister at the end of World War II.

4 ❧ Social Studies

Politics and Government

Booktalk

Bauer, Joan. *Hope Was Here.* New York: G. P. Putnam's Sons, 2000. IL YA, RL 5.1

"Hope Was Here." How many times have I written that? Well, here I am writing it again. And Aunt Addie and I are once again packing up the car and moving. If it weren't for Gleason Beal, things would be different. I trusted him. So did Aunt Addie. Why did he have to steal all our money and skip town? So Aunt Addie, the best diner cook ever, and I are moving to Mulhoney, Wisconsin. Addie has a new job out there at the Welcome Stairs Diner. I'll do some waitressing too. I don't like to brag, but for only being 16 years old, I'm a pretty good waitress. I learned from one of the best—my mother. You see, Addie takes care of me, but she isn't my mother. Deena is. But I haven't seen Deena for a few years. She's waitressing someplace I guess. Whenever I see her, she gives me great tips on how to be a better waitress. So I'll use my skills and try to be the best waitress the town has ever seen. This time, things will be different. You think all teenagers care about are musicians and movie stars? Spend some time in Wisconsin. We'll blow your socks off!

Learning Extension Ideas

1. Have students create a campaign slogan for the mayoral race described in the book. Choose either candidate, and create a campaign poster for him.

2. Hope has changed her name from the one that was given to her at birth. Ask students: If you were to change your name, what would it be? Why?

Booktalk

Haddix, Margaret Peterson. *Among the Hidden.* New York: Simon & Schuster, 1998. IL 5–8, RL 4.7

Luke is a Shadow Child. He hasn't heard the term yet, but he will. Luke is living in a future time where the Population Police rule family life. It is the law that families can only have two children. Luke has two older brothers, so he must remain hidden from everyone and everything. He doesn't quite know what will happen to him if he is found out, but he is sure his parents would be punished. Meanwhile, life isn't too bad. Luke can work on his father's farm and get out into the sunshine. But when the woods are cut down to make room for some fancy new houses, Luke is restricted to the house all the time. He finds that he can peek out of the attic vent and see the new houses. What he sees will change his life forever. To discover what Luke finds in the house of the Baron, read *Among the Hidden.*

Learning Extension Ideas

1. In this story, the government has made laws about how many children couples can have. There are people who believe the government should not interfere with families or be allowed to dictate. This book examines the fine line between basic rights and privileges. Have students prepare a debate topic that will examine whether having a family is a right or a privilege. What are some of the points to be made on each side of the argument? Are there governments today that restrict reproduction?

2. Often when there is a political protest, the protest is literally written on the walls. Have students look around their town to see if they can spot political graffiti on any buildings or walls or even rocks. Have them keep a journal noting the wording of the graffiti and what they think it means. Ask them: Can you tell anything about your town by what is written on the walls?

3. Have students write a new ending for the story, or add an extra chapter. They must use a similar style and the ending has to make sense with the rest of the story.

Booktalk

Lowry, Lois. *Gathering Blue.* Boston: Houghton Mifflin, 2000. IL 5–8, RL 6.3

Kira waits alone in the fields with the body of her mother. It is the custom. Someone must sit by the body for four days to help the spirit find its way from the body. Now that she is alone, Kira wonders what life will be like. Her father died before she was born, so it's been just Kira and her mother. When she returns to the village, she is told that she is to be driven from the village and given to the Beasts. After all, she should never have been allowed to live in the first place. She was born with a deformed leg. Everyone knows that she should have been brought to the fields for the Beasts to consume. Kira's mother had been brave enough to stand up to those in power and had convinced them that Kira should be allowed to live. But now Kira is alone and there is no one to stand up for her. In addition, Vandara has her mind set on taking Kira's land. She's got the other women convinced that the girl with the bad leg would be nothing but a burden to all. When the matter is brought to the Council of Guardians, Kira finds an unexpected protector. But is he all that he seems? Is he helping Kira, or does he have something else in mind? Why is he so interested in her skill with embroidery? To find out, read *Gathering Blue*.

Learning Extension Ideas

1. In this novel, the government has banned the general public from knowing how to read. Ask students: Why would a government do that? What advantages or disadvantages do the people in power gain by not allowing the citizens to have easy access to the society's history?

2. Ask students: Why did the people in power create the story about the beasts? Do you think they knew the true story of what was happening? What would the people do if they knew about the other colony?

3. Ask students: Why do you think Kira made the decision she did? Would you have made a different decision?

Booktalk

Nixon, Joan Lowery. *A Candidate for Murder.* New York: Dell, 1991. IL YA, RL 5.4

Maybe you know someone like Cary. Cary is 16—just an average girl with a boyfriend and lots of other friends. But things are about to change drastically for her. Cary's father just announced that he is a candidate to be the next governor of Texas. The crowds of people who come around become intolerable for Cary, so she visits a friend to get away from all the chaos at her own home. Soon she realizes that she is being followed. Not only that, but someone keeps calling in the middle of the night. This is not standard treatment for a politician's daughter. Who can be doing these things? Is there more that she should be aware of? Cary sets out to find out who is doing this to her and why. What she doesn't know is that she is *A Candidate for Murder*.

Learning Extension Ideas

1. Cary is being followed and is awakened in the night by mysterious phone calls. She knows that this is not the normal life of a politician's daughter. Have students research what life is like for a governor and the governor's family. Ask them: Can you find any information about the governor's children? Write a daily diary entry for the daughter of a governor.

2. Have students create a schedule for a politician's family member during election time. Should he or she be expected to campaign as much as the candidate? Why?

Booktalk

Temple, Frances. *Taste of Salt: The Story of Modern Haiti.* New York: HarperTrophy, 1994. IL YA, RL 7.2

It's hard to believe that in modern Haiti people are forced to harvest crops in Honduras, are made to incur heavy debt at the company store for subsistence food supplies, and are paid so poorly that they can never pay off their debt or regain their liberty to leave. On his hospital bed, Djo tells the story of how he escaped this life and became a worker for President Aristide. Djo was brought up in the middle class of Haiti. One of "Titid's boys" he was a vital member of Aristide's election team. He fought to overthrow the military dictatorship in Haiti. Now he is paying for that fight. He'll tell you his story. You can also meet Jeremie, who has a story of her own. She grew up in the slums of Haiti. She knows firsthand how difficult life can be. And then there's Jean-Bertrand Aristide himself. He has a dream for a new Haiti. He wants to create a society where all have enough to eat, a roof over their heads, and jobs to go to. How do these stories fit together? Find out and learn about life in Haiti in *Taste of Salt.*

Learning Extension Ideas

1. Ask students: What does the title of this book mean? What is the taste of salt?

2. Have students research Haiti. Ask them: After Aristide was removed from office, what happened to him? What happened in Haiti? What are the current conditions in Haiti? Is it still under a dictatorship, or has democracy been restored?

3. It takes a special breed of person to work for the overthrow of the government. Ask students: In this case, was Djo involved in treason? Why or why not?

Booktalk

Yolen, Jane, and Bruce Coville. *Armageddon Summer.* San Diego: Harcourt Brace, 1998. IL YA, RL 5.2

The world will end on July 27, 2000. At least that's what Marina's mother believes. Why would God choose Marina's birthday to end the world? It doesn't seem quite fair to Marina, but she and her family belong to Reverend Beelson's Believers, and that's what he believes. Reverend Beelson takes the congregation to the top of a mountain in western Massachusetts, where exactly 144 Believers will be saved. In addition to the members of Marina's church, there are also Believers from Boston who join the group. Jed is not quite a Believer, but he needs to stay with his father. What happens to the people on the mountain awaiting the end of the world? Read *Armageddon Summer* to find out!

Learning Extension Ideas

1. The United States was founded on the principle of separation of church and state. In this book, the church has convinced the followers to forsake society to create a new world order. Ask students: Should the government have stepped in to protect the Believers? Have a class discussion and debate the issue.

2. Jed gets his information from the Internet and from the radio. Have students create a radio talk show where you are interviewing a member of the Believers and a family member who was not going to the mountain. Conduct dialog between them. Also have call-ins from listeners.

Suggested Further Reading

Bonners, Susan. *Edwina Victorious.* New York: Farrar, Straus & Giroux, 2000. IL 3–6, RL 4.6

Edwina follows in the footsteps of her namesake great-aunt when she begins to write letters to the mayor about community problems and poses as Edwina the elder.

Gutman, Dan. *The Kid Who Ran for President.* New York: Scholastic, ©1996. IL 5–8, RL 6.2

With his friend as campaign manager and his former babysitter as running mate, 12-year-old Judson Moon sets out to become president of the United States.

Haas, Jessie. *Will You, Won't You?* New York: Greenwillow Books, ©2000. IL 5–8, RL 6.5

Spending the summer with her strong-willed politician grandmother, 14-year-old Mad achieves breakthroughs in both her horseback riding and her Scottish dancing and begins to develop the self-confidence she has always lacked.

Hurwitz, Johanna. *Class President.* New York: Morrow Junior Books, ©1990. IL 3–6, RL 4.3

Julio hides his own leadership ambitions to help another candidate win the nomination for class president.

Klee, Sheila. *Volunteering for a Political Campaign.* New York: Children's Press, ©2000. IL YA

Klee discusses the concept of service learning, in which young people gain knowledge and skills through volunteer work, and looks at how the concept applies to political campaigns.

Lewis, Barbara A. *The Kid's Guide to Social Action: How to Solve the Social Problems You Choose—And Turn Creative Thinking into Positive Action.* Minneapolis, Minn.: Free Spirit, ©1998. IL 5–8, RL 7.5

This resource guide for children teaches political action skills that can help kids make a difference in solving social problems at the community, state, and national levels.

Sobel, Syl. *Presidential Elections and Other Cool Facts.* Hauppauge, N.Y.: Barron's Educational Series, ©2000. IL 3–6, RL 5.1

Sobel examines how U.S. presidents are elected and includes some facts about the men elected.

Temple, Frances. *The Beduins' Gazelle.* New York: Orchard Books, ©1996. IL 5–8, RL 6.7

In 1302, two cousins of the nomadic Beni Khalid tribe who are betrothed become separated by political intrigue between warring tribes.

Vail, Rachel. *Popularity Contest.* New York: Scholastic, ©2000. IL 5–8, RL 5.5

Zoe tries to run for class president, but her friendships, crushes, and everyday worries always seem to interfere with her campaign.

Williams, Laura E. *Up a Creek.* New York: Henry Holt, 2001. IL 5–8, RL 5.8

Thirteen-year-old Starshine Bott learns how to cope with an unconventional, politically active mother and does a lot of growing up in the process.

Personal Issues

Booktalk

Anderson, Laurie Halse. *Speak.* New York: Farrar, Straus & Giroux, 1999. IL YA, RL 7.1

On the first day of school the freshmen are all herded into the auditorium. The kids separate into their own cliques. Everyone seems to have someone to sit with. Everyone except Melinda. She had been looking forward to starting high school with her friends. But now, after that night in August, no one wants to be seen with her. How could she have done it? What a stupid thing to do. Now Melinda faces being an outcast. She faces the taunts and stares from kids who used to be her friends. None of them really knows what happened during that party. Melinda certainly can't tell anyone. As the school year goes on, Melinda becomes more and more quiet. She doesn't really see much point in speaking about anything. The only place Melinda feels safe is in art class. Mr. Freeman has assigned each student an object to draw all year long. Melinda gets a tree. We see Melinda's tree grow and evolve as Melinda grows and comes to terms with her emotions. Will Melinda find the courage she needs to speak the truth? Will anyone believe her if she does?

> ➤ **NOTE:** This book may be too intense for younger students. Teachers are advised to read the book carefully before suggesting it to students.

Learning Extension Ideas

1. Ask students: Do you think Melinda was right to call the police? Why or why not?

2. Have students write a letter to Melinda after they find out what happened to her. Ask them: What do you want to tell her? Can you understand what she when through? Can you relate it to something in your own life?

3. Have students describe a time that they looked forward to when they were sure things were going to turn out great but they didn't. They should then contrast it with a time they thought things would turn out bad but they actually turned out really well.

Booktalk

Garden, Nancy. *Holly's Secret.* New York: Farrar, Straus & Giroux, 2000. IL 3–6, RL 5.5

Today my name is Holly Lawrence-Jones. But this is the last day that Holly will exist. Starting tomorrow, I will become Yvette Lawrence-Jones. Life seemed okay when we lived in New York, but now that we live in western Massachusetts, things are different. I want to be from a normal home. I don't want to be an adopted kid living with two mothers. I hear the kids at school talking about fags and dykes, and I don't want them to use those words about us. I just want to be a normal kid living with a normal family. I know it will hurt my moms, but I just need to do this. So, out with Holly and in with Yvette. Which one do you think will be the more popular? Which one do you think I will choose to be?

Learning Extension Ideas

1. Every family is different, but each is special in its own way. Have students explore what makes their families special. Are there special traditions or customs that are unique to their families?

2. Have students take on new personas the way Holly did and write about their new identities. Ask them: What is your new name? Why? How would you act? What is different about you?

Booktalk

Klass, David. *You Don't Know Me.* New York: Farrar, Straus & Giroux, 2001. IL YA, RL 5.0

You don't know me. You might think you do. You see what you think is an average boy in an average town. But what you don't know is that this place is not really what you think it is. Every day I go to the place that is not a school. I sit in algebra class that is not algebra class. I talk to people who are not really anything like they think. I live in a home that is not a home with my mom and a man who is not my father.

John lives in a world that none of us knows. His world is not exactly like the one we live in. On the outside, he appears to be a normal teenager. But on the inside, he has experiences that none of us can know. His tuba is not a tuba to him. It's a giant bullfrog that is waiting to get away. As the year progresses, John slowly spirals out of control to the point where his two worlds begin to meld. What is going on in John's life that makes him want to live in a made-up one? Can anyone help him? Can anyone really get to know him? To find out, read *You Don't Know Me*.

Learning Extension Ideas

1. In this book, John sees things differently than others do. His tuba is a giant bullfrog; he makes up names for people that he feels reflect their personalities. Have students come up with alternate names for common items that reflect their use or appearance.

2. Have students write a personal description of things they are not. They should end the description with a positive item about what they are.

Booktalk

Powell, Randy. *Tribute to Another Dead Rock Star.* New York: Farrar, Straus & Giroux, 1999. IL YA, RL 4.4

I'm sure you have all heard of the death of a famous rock star. Be it Kurt Cobain or John Lennon or Jerry Garcia, the death of a celebrity hits us all in different ways. Some of us tend to take it personally. Even though we have never met these people and don't really know about their private lives, we might think we know them and we feel a loss. After Kurt Cobain's death, thousands of fans flocked to Seattle to pay tribute to him. Even years after his death, people continue to visit Elvis Presley's home and feel a link to him. In this story, heavy metal rocker Debbie Grennan has been dead for three years, but the world is still listening to her songs. When a famous band decides to play a tribute concert to her memory, Debbie's 15-year-old son Grady is asked to participate. Grady agrees to do the morning radio show and is excited about the concert that night. He is looking forward to hanging out with the band. It's not his favorite band, but his half-brother Louie is a big fan. Oh yes, Louie. I forgot to mention him. He's mentally retarded and he lives with his father and stepmother nearby. Grady is living with his grandmother for now, but he knows that won't last. Grady loves Louie but finds it hard to visit him. Grady doesn't get along with Louie's stepmother one bit. They argue about everything. Grady wants Louie to come to the concert tonight, but he knows there will be a terrible argument about it. Can Grady convince Louie's stepmother that Louie should be there? Will Grady be able to get through the day without breaking down?

Learning Extension Ideas

1. In this book, Grady is at first reluctant to participate in yet another tribute to his dead mother. Whenever celebrities die, the public begins to create legends about them. Impromptu shrines are erected and some people devote their lives to keeping their idols' memories alive. Ask students: Why do you think that is? What type of person is involved with this type of activity?

2. Have students write a story about a celebrity they admire. Ask students: What is it about that person that makes him or her worthy of your attention? What has he or she achieved that is worthy? Do you think you really know what this person is like? Have you ever heard or read anything about this person that differs from your view of him or her?

Booktalk

Spinelli, Jerry. *Stargirl.* New York: Alfred A. Knopf, 2000. IL 5–8, RL 6.1

Have you seen her? What about you? Did you see her? If you have to ask who, then you definitely haven't seen her. They say she's a product of home schooling gone bad. She dresses like she's right out of a TV western. And, you won't believe this, she carries a rat with her everywhere she goes! Did you hear what she did in the cafeteria today? She got up and started playing a ukulele! She danced around the room playing and singing, "I'm looking over a four leaf clover!" Have you ever seen anything so weird? She calls herself Stargirl. I've heard that isn't her real name, just the one she made up for herself. She plays her ukulele and sings during lunch. She cheers the other team during games. She goes to funerals for people she doesn't even know. How can she ever fit into our school? How could we be expected to accept someone so different? What do you think? Could you look beyond the weirdness to find the girl within? Would you risk your social standing to befriend a girl like *Stargirl*?

Learning Extension Ideas

1. In the novel, Stargirl is portrayed as very different from the other students. We often view people as different, but once we get to know them, we find we have many things in common. Find out who in the class has things in common. Read statements and ask any student to whom the statement applies to stand up. Some examples are: "I was born in [August]," "My favorite food is [ice cream]," "My favorite television show is [. . .]." What does this tell you about the students in the class?

2. Stargirl decides to try to be like everyone else so that she can be popular. Ask students: Did it work? Why or why not? Have students rewrite the ending of the book to show what may have happened to Stargirl.

Booktalk

Strasser, Todd. *Give a Boy a Gun.* New York: Simon & Schuster Books for Young Readers, 1999. IL 5–8, RL 6.4

Do you know someone in your class who is the target of bullies? Someone who is always teased, pushed, called names, and generally picked on? Have you ever wondered what that person's life might be like? Have you ever tried to put yourself into his or her shoes? Consider Gary and Brendan as they go from seventh grade through tenth grade. They are outsiders. They aren't accepted by the "in-crowd." Their daily school life is filled with name calling, pushing, and ridicule. They feel helpless to stop it. The teachers don't seem to want to help. Their parents aren't in a position to put an end to it. Gary and Brendan just know that they can't go on another two years in school being tortured. They need to do something. Something big. Could they possibly think that destroying the "in-crowd" kids would serve any purpose? Can they pull it off? Should they? Find out what happens when you *Give a Boy a Gun.*

➤ **NOTE:** This book may be too intense for younger students. Teachers are advised to read the book carefully before suggesting it to students.

Learning Extension Ideas

1. This book touches on a topic of major importance. Have students participate in a roundtable discussion about school violence. Ask them: What are the issues? What can be done?

2. Have students write an intervention letter about a hypothetical situation in which they notice a friend is exhibiting the early warning signs of violence.

3. Have students research school violence in other countries. Compare the number of incidents to those in the United States. Create a map displaying school violence statistics in other countries. What can the class conclude from this?

Booktalk

Walker, Kate. *Peter.* Boston: Houghton Mifflin, 1993. IL YA, RL 5.3

Peter Dawson is just an average 15-year-old boy. He loves dirt biking and fast cars and even has his own darkroom to use. But he has never been comfortable around girls and he begins to think there must be something wrong with him. When he finds himself becoming attracted to David, he really gets worried. David is his brother's best friend—and he is gay. Does that mean that Peter is gay? Peter feels totally alone in his doubts. He can't tell anyone about how he is feeling. He has no one to turn to—or does he? Join Peter on his search for identity. Will he be able to sort out his feelings? Can he come to terms with what he learns?

Learning Extension Ideas

1. Peter feels he has no one to talk to about his feelings and confusion. There are many places that he could have gone to find someone to talk to. Have students research their community and find places that Peter could have turned to. Students can compile a list of helpful organizations.

2. Have students write a self-help pamphlet with information about teenage issues. Include addresses of helpful organizations, Web pages, and books that students can use to find answers.

Suggested Further Reading

Conly, Jane Leslie. *Crazy Lady!* New York: HarperCollins, 1993. IL 5–8, RL 4.9

As he tries to come to terms with his mother's death, Vernon finds solace in his growing relationship with the neighborhood outcasts, an alcoholic and her retarded son.

Gantos, Jack. *Joey Pigza Swallowed the Key.* New York: Farrar, Straus & Giroux, 1998. IL 5–8, RL 5.2

To the constant disappointment of his mother and his teachers, Joey has trouble paying attention and controlling his mood swings when his prescription medications wear off and he starts getting worked up and acting wired.

Haddix, Margaret Peterson. *Don't You Dare Read This,* *Mrs. Dunphrey.* New York: Simon & Schuster Books for Young Readers, ©1996. IL 5–8, RL 6.2

In the journal she is keeping for English class, 16-year-old Tish chronicles the changes in her life when her abusive father abandons her and her brother, and her mother follows him.

Hahn, Mary Downing. *Following My Own Footsteps.* New York: Clarion Books, ©1996. IL 5–8, RL 4.8

In 1945, Gordy's grandmother takes him and his family into her North Carolina home after his abusive father is arrested. He is just beginning to respond to his grandmother's loving discipline when his father returns.

Kerr, M. E. *Deliver Us from Evie.* New York: HarperTrophy, 1995. IL YA, RL 6.5

Sixteen-year-old Parr Burrman and his family face some difficult times when word spreads through their rural Missouri town that his older sister is a lesbian. Then she leaves the family farm to live with the daughter of the town's banker.

Myers, Anna. *When the Bough Breaks.* New York: Walker, 2000. IL 5–8, RL 6.2

Fifteen-year-old Ophelia, orphaned and emotionally isolated, develops an unlikely friendship with an elderly recluse, Portia McKay, that may lead to redemption for both.

Neufeld, John. *Almost a Hero.* New York: Atheneum Books for Young Readers, ©1995. IL 5–8, RL 7.0

Twelve-year-old Ben Derby spends his spring break volunteering at a Santa Barbara day care center for homeless children.

Philbrick, W. R. *Freak the Mighty.* New York: Scholastic, ©1993. IL 5–8, RL 6.3

At the beginning of eighth grade, learning disabled Max and his new friend Freak, whose birth defect has affected his body but not his brilliant mind, find that when they combine forces they make a powerful team.

Vande Velde, Vivian. *Alison, Who Went Away.* Boston: Houghton Mifflin, 2001. IL 5–8, RL 5.2

Three years after the disappearance of her older sister, 14-year-old Sibyl and her family struggle to continue their lives, separately and together.

Werlin, Nancy. *Are You Alone on Purpose?* Boston: Houghton Mifflin, 1994. IL 5–8, RL 5.6

When two lonely teenagers, one the son of a widower rabbi and the other the sister of an autistic twin, are drawn together by a tragic accident, they discover they have more in common than they guessed.

Children with Disabilities

Booktalk

Anderson, Rachel. *The Bus People.* New York: Henry Holt, 1992. IL 5–8, RL 5.5

Every day, Bertram climbs aboard the school bus and sets off to collect his riders. He doesn't mind this route. It's one that few drivers want. It's the "fruit-cake-bus." Some of the kids can't talk; some can't walk. But Bertram believes they are all special in their own way. He tries to look beyond the kids' handicaps to see the children within. He sees Rebecca, who dreams of being her sister's bridesmaid, and Micky, who is trapped inside a useless body but longs to leave home. Each child has a story. Ride along with Bertram and meet the kids on the bus.

Learning Extension Ideas

1. Students often do not understand how difficult it is for physically and/or mentally disabled students to get around in school. Have students experience what it is to have a handicap and then write about their experiences. Some children can be blindfolded, some can wear earplugs, some can use a wheelchair. To simulate a learning disability, students can try writing with their nondominant hand. Have students discuss how people might have to compensate for a disability.

2. Have students brainstorm ways to help disabled students. What can they do to make it a bit easier for someone who is struggling?

Booktalk

Gantos, Jack. *Joey Pigza Loses Control.* New York: Farrar, Straus & Giroux, 2000. IL 5–8, RL 5.9

You may have already met Joey Pigza. He's a boy who just can't control himself. He wants to be good but just can't do what he knows he should. Well, in the first book Joey is diagnosed with ADHD and put on medication. It seems to be working and Joey is not nearly as wired as he used to be. He and his mother remember those days and are so happy that the new medications are working well. Nothing is perfect, of course. When Joey's mother leaves him alone during summer vacation, his impulses cause a bit of trouble. It seems Joey just can't be left on his own. It is decided that he will go to spend the summer with his father. Joey hasn't seen his father in years and can't really remember what he is like. Joey's mother has told him that Carter Pigza is just a grown-up version of Joey. When Joey finally meets his father, Carter doesn't seem so bad. He is pretty wired, but that's to be expected. When Joey's father decides that Joey doesn't need to be on medication anymore, he flushes it all down the toilet. Can Joey keep the old wired self away? Can he really be a normal boy?

Learning Extension Ideas

1. Have students do a quickwrite about what they know about Attention Deficit Hyperactivity Disorder (ADHD). Have they ever known anyone with Attention Deficit Disorder (ADD)? Have they ever seen that person when he or she was not on medication? How was the person different?

2. Have students imagine that Joey decides to write a letter to Dear Abby when he realizes that he is losing control. They should write the letter for him and answer these questions: What advice would he be asking for? How would he describe what he was going through? What would Abby reply?

Booktalk

Helfman, Elizabeth S. *On Being Sarah.* Morton Grove, Ill.: Whitman, 1993. IL 5–8, RL 4.9

Sarah is 12 years old and has cerebral palsy, which limits what she can do. She is confined to a wheelchair and can't talk. In spite of her handicap, Sarah goes to school on her own and attends mainstream classes. She uses a special motorized wheelchair to get around. To communicate with others, she uses Blissymbols. Sarah tells us about her life, her hopes, and her first "friend who happens to be a boy."

Learning Extension Ideas

1. Sarah is able to attend classes and communicate with others by using adaptive technology. Have students research adaptive technology and explain how the different devices can help handicapped students obtain an education.

2. Have students design a product that could help a student with a disability. The product doesn't need to be realistic. The students should tell what the device is intended to do and how it will improve the life of a handicapped student.

Booktalk

Kehret, Peg. *Small Steps: The Year I Got Polio.* Morton Grove, Ill.: Whitman, 1998. IL 3–6, RL 5.6 (Nonfiction)

I'm sure you know what it's like when you are waiting for something big to happen. Time just seems to stand still. Well, that is just how Peg feels. She can't wait until the end of the school day. This is Homecoming day, and the seventh grade float is sure to win first place. During chorus, Peg's leg keeps twitching and she can't seem to get it to stop. On her way out of class, she is embarrassed when her leg gives out and she falls down. Her books fly all over the place! When Peg goes home for lunch, her mother notices that Peg feels hot. She calls the doctor. It is then that Peg knows there was no use begging to go to Homecoming. All she can think about doing is sleeping, anyway. After the doctor examines her, he tells her parents to get her to the hospital—Peg has polio.

Learning Extension Ideas

1. Author Peg Kehret tells us about her struggle to overcome a major illness. Overcoming a bad situation often makes us stronger people. Have students write about a struggle in their lives that they overcame. What did they learn about themselves from this?

2. Have students write a letter to the author telling her how they felt about this book. Did it leave them with any questions? If so, they should ask Ms. Kehret.

Booktalk

O'Connor, Barbara. *Me and Rupert Goody.* New York: Farrar, Straus & Giroux, 1999. IL 5–8, RL 6.0

Jennalee Helton, age 11, lives in North Carolina's Great Smoky Mountains. She comes from a very large family but feels alone most of the time. Even when she is fighting for a bed to sleep in, she feels all alone. No one really notices her, except Beauregard Goody. Uncle Beau, as he is known, owns the local general store. Here, Jennalee spends hours feeling that she belongs somewhere. Uncle Beau and Jennalee have their own routine that gives her a sense of security. All this changes when Rupert Goody shows up. Who is he?

All that is certain is that he is mentally handicapped. Is he really who he says he is? And how will his relationship with Uncle Beau change Jennalee's life?

Learning Extension Ideas

1. Ask students: How did Jennalee's feelings about Rupert change as she got to know him? Why was she unhappy when he first appeared?

2. Rupert is mentally handicapped. Ask students: How does that fact affect the way people treated him when he first appeared in town? Do you think things would have been different if Rupert did not have a disability?

Booktalk

Trueman, Terry. *Stuck in Neutral.* New York: HarperCollins, 2000. IL 5–8, RL 6.7

Hi. My name is Shawn McDaniel. I'm 14 years old. I live with my mother, sister, and brother. My dad left a few years ago, but he is still in the picture. There's a lot of love in my life. I love to read. I love to listen to music. I love to look at girls! You might say I'm a perfectly normal 14-year-old boy. Well, you might say that, if you knew me. Really knew me. Unfortunately, no one really knows me. Not my family. Not my teachers. No one can ever really know me. You see, when I was born, a freaky thing happened to me. A blood vessel in my brain burst. And it just so happens that it was in exactly the right spot to make it impossible for me to control my muscles. I can't walk or talk or even blink when I want. I sit in a wheelchair playing Bing-Bong the Idiot-Puppet-boy. I can't even control swallowing, so I drool too much. I'm not surprised that people don't know there is a real person inside this body. Oh yeah, I also have seizures. I have several each day. I kind of enjoy them. I know that sounds strange, but I really do. They sort of let me escape from my body for a few minutes. Unfortunately, people think I'm in pain when I have my seizures. My dad certainly does. I can see the sadness in his eyes—at least when I happen to be able to look in his direction. His sadness seems to be leading him in a direction I don't think I want him to take. You see, lately I've come to believe that my father has decided to end my pain by killing me. Can I even hope that he will realize that I'm actually quite happy in here? Should I be afraid? I just don't know. After all, I'm just *Stuck in Neutral.*

Learning Extension Ideas

1. The author keeps us in the dark about how this story ends. Have students write their own ending. They should explain why they think the book ends that way.

2. Have students search newspapers and magazines, editorials, cartoons, and the Internet for information about mercy killing [or find another term to describe it: euthanasia, assisted suicide, etc.] Ask them what point of view the items they find are presented from. Create a bulletin board display of the articles. Group them into categories: pro, con, neutral.

Suggested Further Reading

Burnett, Frances Hodgson. *The Secret Garden.* New York: HarperCollins, 1990. IL 5–8, RL 6.8

Ten-year-old Mary comes to live in a lonely house on the Yorkshire moors and discovers a disabled cousin and the mysteries of a locked garden.

Farrell, Mame. *Marrying Malcolm Murgatroyd.* New York: Farrar, Straus & Giroux, 1995. IL 5–8, RL 6.0

Hannah Billings hates being teased about marrying Malcolm Murgatroyd, the most unpopular and misunderstood boy in her sixth-grade class. That is, until he reveals his true personality when her brother succumbs to muscular dystrophy.

Fletcher, Susan. *Shadow Spinner.* New York: Atheneum Books for Young Readers, ©1998. IL 5–8, RL 5.5

When Marjan, a 13-year-old crippled girl, joins the sultan's harem in ancient Persia, she gathers for Shahrazad the stories that will save the queen's life.

Hatrick, Gloria. *Masks.* New York: Orchard Books, 1996. IL 5–8, RL 5.2

Desperate to help his older brother Will, who has become paralyzed by a rare disease, Pete uses tribal animal masks to communicate with Will. This allows Will to escape his useless body and embark on a series of strange and powerful dream journeys.

Helfman, Elizabeth S. *On Being Sarah.* Morton Grove, Ill.: Whitman, 1993. IL 5–8, RL 4.9

Even though life with cerebral palsy isn't easy for 12-year-old Sarah, she manages with the help of her loving family and several new friends.

Mazer, Harry. *The Wild Kid.* New York: Simon & Schuster Books for Young Readers, ©1998. IL 5–8, RL 3.5

Twelve-year-old Sammy, who is mildly retarded, runs away from home and becomes a prisoner of Kevin, a wild kid living in the woods.

McElfresh, Lynn E. *Can You Feel the Thunder?* New York: Atheneum Books for Young Readers, ©1999. IL 5–8, RL 7.1

Thirteen-year-old Mic Parsons struggles with mixed feelings about his deaf and blind sister while at the same time making his way through the turmoil of junior high.

Mikaelsen, Ben. *Petey.* New York: Hyperion Books for Children, ©1998. IL 5–8, RL 7.0

In 1922 Petey, who has cerebral palsy, is misdiagnosed as an idiot and institutionalized. Sixty years later, still in the institution, he befriends a boy and shares with him the joy of life.

Philbrick, Rodman. *Freak the Mighty.* New York: Scholastic, ©1993. IL 5–8, RL 6.3

Max, a large eighth-grader with a learning disability, becomes friends with Freak, an intelligent boy who is physically impaired.

Roos, Stephen. *The Gypsies Never Came.* New York: Simon & Schuster Books for Young Readers, ©2001. IL 5–8, RL 7.1

Sixth-grader Augie Knapp, who has a deformed hand, is convinced by Lydie Rose, the strange new girl in town, that the gypsies are coming for him.

Multicultural Novels

Booktalk

Choi, Sook Nyul. *Year of Impossible Goodbyes.* Boston: Houghton Mifflin, 1991. IL 5–8, RL 6.3

Life is difficult for 10-year-old Sookan and her family. Living in North Korea during World War II under Japanese rule, they are not allowed to speak Korean or wear their traditional clothing. As the war ends, Sookan hopes life will return to normal, but it doesn't. The Russians move into North Korea, so Sookan and her family decide to escape to South Korea. Sookan and her brother are separated from their mother at the train station and spend days looking for her. After many days, they decide to head for South Korea on their own. Will the children make it to safety? Will they ever see their mother again?

Learning Extension Ideas

1. Ask students: What do you think your life would be like if you were not allowed to speak your native language or wear the clothes you wanted to wear? How do you think you would feel? What do you think you would do?

2. Have students write a letter to Sookan's mother. Ask them: What do you think Sookan would want to tell her mother if she believed she would never see her again? How would she say goodbye?

Booktalk

Crew, Linda. *Children of the River.* New York: Delacorte Press, 1989. IL YA, RL 5.6

Sundara is a good Cambodian girl. She works hard at school and gets good grades. She respects her aunt and uncle, with whom she lives. She works after school on a farm with her family. She's successful; she drives a car and does the grocery shopping. The problem is, she feels guilty because she's starting to break away from her family's rules: strict Cambodian rules about girls not dating boys, family-arranged marriages, no luxuries, and a strong Khmer nationality. Jonathan, a school sports star, becomes interested in Sundara after her English assignment on one of life's problems reveals a hint of the trauma she has lived through. Sundara is a refugee. She escaped without her parents or sisters. She was sent to live with her aunt and uncle because her aunt had just had a baby and needed help. Now, Sundara feels guilty because the baby died. She has no knowledge of her family back home and she is living a very comfortable life here. Even though she likes the young man that the family has arranged for her to marry, she finds herself drawn to Jonathan. In addition to her self-doubt, Sundara's aunt and uncle are disapproving. Can Jonathan be the friend she needs? How can Sundara deal with all that she is going through? Find out what happens to Sundara in *Children of the River.*

Learning Extension Ideas

1. No one suspected the truth about Sundara's background. Often newcomers are avoided and labeled—incorrectly. When people take the time to get to know each other, they often learn that there are more similarities than differences between them. Have students try to find out things that are unique about each other. Each student should write a fact about himself or herself on an index

card. This should be something that students think no one else has experienced. After collecting the cards, read them aloud and have the class try to guess whom each applies to. Did anyone really have a unique experience?

2. Sundara wants to please her aunt and uncle, but she is torn between Cambodian tradition and her American lifestyle. This is often a conflict for immigrants. Should they keep their customs or adapt to the customs of their new home? Ask students: Do you think Sundara should follow her aunt and uncle's wishes, or should she follow her heart?

Booktalk

Ellis, Deborah. *The Breadwinner.* Toronto: Douglas & McIntyre, 2000. IL 5–8, RL 6.1

I can't believe this is happening! Hasn't my life been hard enough? And now this! How can my mother expect me to make such a sacrifice? I remember life before the Taliban. I actually don't remember too much, but I remember that Kabul was a wonderful place to live. We had a big house, and we laughed a lot. Now we live in one room in a bombed-out building. Mother and Nooria never go outside anymore. They simply can't get down the stairs when wearing their burqas (long garments that cover the women completely). They just can't maneuver in them. Since I am only 11, I don't have to completely cover up and I am allowed outside, especially to help my father, who reads letters in the markets to earn money so we can eat. The Taliban government does not value education. Girls are not allowed to go to school. But now my father has been arrested and there is no one to earn money for us. Mother has decided that I must cut my hair, dress as a boy, and become the family's breadwinner.

Learning Extension Ideas

1. Have students brainstorm what they already know about the Afghan region and its history. Ask them: What have you heard in the news recently about Afghanistan? What questions do you have? Why do you think it is beneficial for Americans to understand more about the people and history of Afghanistan at this time?

2. Have students research the rise of the Taliban. Create a timeline of events leading to the Taliban taking control of Afghanistan. Points to include are the war with the Soviets that created the opportunity for the Taliban to take power, destruction of religious sites, the marking of non-Muslims, the treatment of women, and so forth.

3. The tragedy of September 11, 2001, left the world stunned. It also began a series of events that have led to the "War on Terrorism." The invasion of Afghanistan was the first step in this effort. Have students research the main reasons for the United States to become involved in this war. Ask students: How is this war different from others fought by the United States?

Booktalk

Kurtz, Jane. *The Storyteller's Beads.* San Diego: Harcourt Brace, 1998. IL 3–6, RL 5.9

Sahay, a young Ethiopian girl, lives with her uncle after her parents are killed. After the terrible drought in Ethiopia, the villagers struggle to survive. Then enemies arrive to seize their land, and Sahay and her uncle are forced to flee. Many of the Kemant people find themselves in the same predicament: homeless and forced to wander.

In another village lives Rahel, a blind Beta-Israel girl. Some of the villagers call her a Falasha, an evil eye. She and her brother have also been forced from their home to travel the countryside in desperation. The two girls' lives become intertwined when they travel together to a refugee camp in Sudan. Sahay doesn't like Jews and she doesn't want to travel with Rahel and her people, but she reluctantly agrees. When their plans change, Rahel convinces Sahay to pretend to be her sister so that she will be able to go. Will the girls reach safety?

Learning Extension Ideas

1. Ask students: Why were families leaving Ethiopia? Why were they forced to go to Sudan instead of staying in Ethiopia?

2. Have students research past and present conditions on the Internet and at the library to find out. Ask them: Has the situation changed for the people of Ethiopia? Should anything be done to help?

3. Have students create a map of Sahay's travels. Ask them: Where is Ethiopia? Where is Sudan? How far did Sahay travel? Relate that to your town. What town is as far from your house as the distance Sahay traveled? Do you think you could walk that far?

Booktalk

Ryan, Pam Munoz. *Esperanza Rising.* New York: Scholastic, 2000. IL 5–8, RL 6.2

Esperanza has a wonderful life. She is the only child of a wealthy landowner in Mexico. She has everything she wants: a loving family, good friends, beautiful clothes, toys, and lots of servants. Her birthday is coming up, and she knows her father will give her wonderful presents and have a huge party for her as he always does. But Esperanza's life changes when her father is ambushed by bandits and killed. She and her mother must depend on her mean uncles. When Esperanza's mother refuses to marry one of the uncles, he arranges for the ranch to be burned to the ground. Now Esperanza and her mother have nothing but the clothes on their backs. Together with several of their servants, they travel to California to become field hands. What would you do in Esperanza's place? After living a life of privilege, do you think Esperanza can handle what life will offer her as a poor field hand in a new country?

Learning Extension Ideas

1. In the beginning of the book, Ryan makes note of an old Mexican proverb: "The rich person is richer when he becomes poor, than the poor person when he becomes rich." Ask students: What does this proverb mean? Do you agree?

2. When Esperanza and her mother resettle in California, they hear talk of a strike among some of the workers. Ask students: What is a strike? What do the workers hope to accomplish by striking? Each person had to decide whether to take part in the strike. How do you think you would have decided? What are some of the things you would take into consideration?

3. When the workers were talking of striking, it was noted that people were moving in from Oklahoma who would be willing to work for less. Ask students: Why would people from Oklahoma be willing to do that? What was happening in Oklahoma that made residents willing to move to California to work for small wages?

Booktalk

Savin, Marcia. *The Moon Bridge.* New York: Scholastic, 1992. IL 5–8, RL 5.7

During World War II, when the United States was at war with Japan, Japanese Americans came under suspicion. People doubted that their loyalties were with the United States. For fifth grader Mitzi, this leads to being shunned at school. Only one girl, Ruthie, takes a chance and befriends Mitzi. The two girls become close friends. When the president orders all Japanese Americans into resettlement camps, the girls must say goodbye as Mitzi's family loses everything they had worked for. How will Mitzi survive? Will she and Ruthie ever see each other again?

Learning Extension Ideas

1.   Many Japanese families interned in the camps had relatives in Japan. Have students write a "letter home" to relatives in Japan, describing life in the camps. Remember that all letters will be censored to prevent giving away vital war secrets.

2.   Have students take on the role of President Franklin D. Roosevelt. He is faced with the very difficult decision of what to do with the Japanese Americans on the West Coast. They should make their own decisions and defend them.

Booktalk

Smith, Cynthia Leitich. *Rain Is Not My Indian Name.* New York: HarperCollins, 2001. IL YA

"Rain is not my Indian name; not the way people think of Indian names. But I am an Indian and it is the name my parents gave me." So begins the story of 14-year-old Rain, who has just lost her best friend. How does a young girl handle her feelings of loss? Rain finds her truth through the lens of a camera. Hired to photograph the local Indian Camp program, Rain at first tries to be objective and not get involved with the campers. Will her growing awareness of her culture and her experiences at the camp help her come to terms with death? To find out, read *Rain Is Not My Indian Name.*

Learning Extension Ideas

1.   Ask students: Why was Rain not interested in participating in Indian Camp? What did she learn about herself and her culture throughout the course of the book?

2.   Photographers can often see things through their camera lens that they cannot see with the naked eye. Have students create a photo album of the pictures that may have been taken by Rain that summer. Each student can complete one picture with a caption. Combine the pictures into a classroom photograph album.

Booktalk

Soto, Gary. *Living Up the Street.* New York: Dell, 1985. IL YA, RL 7.5 (Nonfiction)

Meet Gary. Gary lives in a Mexican-American barrio. His family is dirt poor. When Gary's not scrounging for nickel-and-dime jobs, he spends long, hot afternoons in the neighborhood park. In school, he's known as a tough guy—a scrapper. Gary hates much of his life: harvesting grapes, slashing cotton plants. He hates the way many Anglos treat him. But Gary has something that money can't buy, and he'll survive. This is Gary's story of survival and triumph.

Learning Extension Ideas

1. The author writes about his life growing up in poverty and facing prejudice every day. Ask students: How was his childhood different from yours? How was it the same?

2. Gary Soto was able to endure a difficult childhood and has now become a well-known author. Have students research more about his life. Working in groups, they should create a mock interview with him, preparing questions and the answers that they think he would give. More information can be found at his Web site, http://www.garysoto.com. Students can send their questions to the author.

Booktalk

Staples, Suzanne Fisher. *Haveli.* New York: Random House, 1995. IL YA, RL 6.7

This house hides a secret room. It is the room where Shabanu hides. Shabanu has fixed up an attic room as her hideaway. She is one of several wives of a very old man, his country wife. She wants only to surround her daughter with beauty and to keep her safe from the other jealous wives. Shabanu's dark exotic manner clearly makes her the husband's favorite, but she wishes she could become invisible. What country is this where Shabanu lives? How was her life in the country different from her life in the city? What are the lifestyles, ethnic prejudices, preferences and values, and expectations that Shabanu lives with?

Learning Extension Ideas

1. Have students draw a picture of what the attic looks like after Shabanu has fixed it up. Ask them: What items has she put in it to make it more her own? If you were fixing up a hiding room for yourself, what items would you include?

2. Have students write a report on the culture of Pakistan to explain what Shabanu's life is like. Include cultural references that show why certain practices are accepted in Pakistan.

Booktalk

Whelan, Gloria. *Homeless Bird.* New York: HarperCollins, 2000. IL 3–6, RL 4.1

Thirteen-year-old Koly lives in a small village in India. She is happy living with her mother, father, and brothers, but her life is about to change forever. Koly's parents tell her that it is time for her to be married. Her father goes in search of a suitable husband. It is the custom in India to arrange marriages. Koly doesn't question this, but she hopes her father will arrange a good marriage. When a husband is found, her future husband's family insists that the wedding ceremony take place in their home. This is unusual, but not unheard of. Koly and her parents travel to the groom's village. When they arrive, things just don't seem right. The parents seem more interested in getting the dowry than they are in meeting Koly. Koly only meets her new husband at the ceremony. He is much younger than they were led to believe, and he seems very sickly. It turns out that the parents only arranged the marriage so that they could get enough money to take their son on a pilgrimage that they hope will cure him. What will happen to Koly? Can she ever hope to find happiness? Read *Homeless Bird* to find out about the customs of India and how a young girl finds herself coping with them.

Learning Extension Ideas

1. Have students make a list of words from the book that are unfamiliar to them, find their meanings, and create a glossary.

2. Ask students to imagine that they are a representative of an international relief organization. They have come to India to help in the city of widows. What can they do to help?

Booktalk

Yep, Laurence. *The Star Fisher.* New York: Morrow, 1991. IL 5–8, RL 6.6

The Lee family has decided to move from Ohio to West Virginia to expand their laundry business. But the Lees are totally unprepared for what they find when they arrive in West Virginia. They have not experienced the prejudice of small town America in the 1930s. The townsfolk are suspicious of the Asian family and refuse to go to their laundry. The Lee children have trouble making friends at school. The townspeople want nothing to do with anyone they see as different from themselves. Will the family ever fit in? Can a small town accept new people who are seen as outsiders? Or will they be forced to give up and move on? Read the *Star Fisher* to find out.

Learning Extension Ideas

1. Ask students: How does prejudice affect our everyday lives? How does it show itself in our schools, our communities, and our country? What do you think is the cause of prejudice in America?

2. Have students create a survey to distribute in your school on the issue of prejudice. Analyze and graph the results.

3. Have students search magazines and newspapers for articles about incidents involving prejudice. Ask them: How hard is it to find them? Why has the government cracked down on "hate crimes?" How can courts determine whether a violent act is racially motivated?

Suggested Further Reading

Banks, Lynne Reid. *One More River.* New York: Avon, 1993, ©1992. IL 5–8, RL 6.9

Fourteen-year-old Lesley is upset when her parents abandon their comfortable life in Canada for a kibbutz in Israel prior to the 1967 war.

Bernardo, Anilu. *Jumping Off to Freedom.* Houston, Tex.: Pinata Books, 1996. IL YA

Courage and desperation lead 15-year-old David and his father to flee Cuba's repressive regime and seek freedom by taking to the sea on a raft headed for Miami.

Feder, Harriet K. *Mystery of the Kaifeng Scroll: A Vivi Hartman Adventure.* Minneapolis, Minn.: Lerner, ©1995. IL 5–8, RL 4.1

Fifteen-year-old Aviva travels to Istanbul to vacation with her mother. When she arrives to find her mother missing, Vivi must trust an Arab girl, as well as her own knowledge of the Torah, to unravel the mystery.

Naidoo, Beverley. *Chain of Fire.* New York: HarperCollins, 1993. IL 5–8, RL 6.9

When the villagers of Bophelong are forced to leave their houses and resettle in a barren "homeland," 13-year-old Naledi and her schoolmates organize an anti-removal march through their village.

Rankin, Louise. *Daughter of the Mountains.* New York: Puffin Books, 1993. IL 5–8, RL 6.8

Momo undertakes a dangerous journey from the mountains of Tibet to the city of Calcutta, in search of her stolen dog Pempa.

Saldana, Rene. *The Jumping Tree: A Novel.* New York: Delacorte Press, ©2001. IL 5–8, RL 5.9

Rey, a Mexican American living with his closeknit family in a Texas town near the Mexican border, describes his transition from boy to young man.

Soto, Gary. *Local News.* San Diego: Harcourt Brace Jovanovich, ©1993. IL 5–8, RL 5.9

A collection of 13 short stories about the everyday lives of Mexican-American young people in California's Central Valley.

Wartski, Maureen Crane. *A Boat to Nowhere.* New York: Penguin, 1981, ©1980. IL 5–8, RL 5.6

Fleeing from agents of the new communist government in Vietnam, an old man and three children begin a seemingly endless and hopeless struggle for survival as boat people.

Whitesel, Cheryl Aylward. *Rebel: A Tibetan Odyssey.* New York: HarperCollins, ©2000. IL 5–8, RL 5.7

Although he rebels against life in the Tibetan Buddhist monastery where he has been sent, 14-year-old Thunder comes to some amazing realizations about himself.

Wojciechowska, Maia. *Shadow of a Bull.* New York: Atheneum Books for Young Readers, 1983, ©1964. IL 5–8, RL 5.8

Manolo Olivar has to make a decision whether to follow in his famous father's shadow and become a bullfighter or follow his heart and become a doctor.

5 ❦ Language Arts and Literature

Introduction

The importance of studying language arts cannot be overstated. Language is the defining characteristic of human beings. Humans use language to communicate thoughts, ideas, and beliefs and to pass down information through the generations. A knowledgeable and proficient user of language will have an easier time succeeding in school. The command of language follows all through one's lifetime. Competent users of language participate in society as informed citizens. They appreciate and contribute to our culture. Competent users are able to pursue their own goals and interests as independent learners.

Good books are what language arts and literature are all about, and booktalking is a natural in these subject areas. The books help us see our society and our response to it. This chapter covers the classics, some contemporary realistic fiction, adventure books, mystery stories, and fantasy novels.

The Classics

Booktalk

Gipson, Fred. *Old Yeller.* New York: HarperTrophy, 1990. IL 5–8, RL 5.4

Life on the prairie has settled into a routine for the Coates family. While his father is away, Travis has taken over the job of plowing the field. It's rough going. Out of nowhere, a big, ugly dog chases a rabbit through the cornfield, frightening the mule, which then breaks down the fence and tramples the plants! Travis chases the dog away only to find it raiding the smokehouse later. What a pest! Travis decides he must shoot the dog to be rid of it, but his younger brother begs to be allowed to keep it for a pet. Old Yeller proves his worth over and over during the next few weeks by keeping the family safe. But he hasn't changed his old ways. He is still raiding neighboring hen

---

RL = Reading Level   *IL = Interest Level*

81

houses and ruining crops. Will Travis be able to keep Old Yeller? Will he become the pet the boys hope for?

Learning Extension Ideas

1. Farm life can be difficult even today. Travis's father left Travis in charge of the farm while he was away. Ask students: Was that too much responsibility for a 14-year-old? Was Travis prepared for what happened? Have students write a paragraph explaining their thoughts on this.

2. Give the students quotes from the novel and have them write their own responses to those quotes. Go over the quotes in class and have students discuss their responses.

Booktalk

Kipling, Rudyard. *The Jungle Book.* New York: Alfred A. Knopf, 1994. IL 5–8, RL 6.3

Mowgli is lost in the jungles of India. He is just an infant and, of course, there is no way he can survive on his own. Or is there? He crawls into the den of Mother and Father Wolf, who take him in and raise him as their own. He is also befriended by a fun-loving bear. Mowgli's adventures in nineteenth-century India are filled with unexpected troubles and well-learned lessons. Discover why this classic book has endured through the generations.

Learning Extension Ideas

1. *The Jungle Book* is actually several stories in one. Have the students create a timeline showing the different stages of Mowgli's life. They should annotate it to show significant events (e.g., *Infant:* Mowgli crawls into the den of Mother and Father Wolf. *Eight years old:* Mowgli is captured by the Monkey People).

2. The author lived in India as a child. His love of the country shows in his writing. Have the students research Kipling's life and compare events in his life with events depicted in his books.

Booktalk

Montgomery, Lucy Maude. *Anne of Green Gables.* New York: Alfred A. Knopf, 1995. IL 5–8, RL 7.2

Marilla Cuthbert cannot believe her eyes when her brother returns with a red-headed girl in the wagon. Matthew was supposed to get a boy. The brother and sister had decided that since they had no children of their own and they were getting older, taking in an orphan would be just the thing to help them with work around their home. And now Matthew has brought home a girl. Not just any girl, though. Anne is a dramatic, vocal young lady with an imagination that won't quit. And although Anne always tries to do the right thing, she often only succeeds in creating chaos, like the time she accidentally dies her hair green, or the time she mistook wine for juice. But that's just the beginning. Now only one thing is certain: Anne will liven things up around Green Gables. Discover the stories that have charmed readers like you for generations.

Learning Extension Ideas

1. Anne talks about finding a kindred spirit. Have students write about someone in their lives that they consider a kindred spirit.

2. Read the section about the party that Anne attends. Ask students: How would a party you go to be different? What kinds of activities would you take part in? Would it make a difference if the party were all girls or boys or both were invited? Why?

3. Anne loves poetry. Have the students retell the story in poem form. This poem should have a minimum of four stanzas. They can present their poems to the class, adding background music if they like, or present them as a rap.

Suggested Further Reading

Alcott, Louisa May. *Little Women*. New York: Puffin Books, 1997, ©1868. IL 5–8, RL 7.9

Chronicles the joys and sorrows of the four March sisters as they grow into young women in nineteenth-century New England at the time of the Civil War. Includes illustrated notes throughout the text explaining the historical background of the story.

Baum, L. Frank. *The Wizard of Oz*. New York: Aladdin Paperbacks, 1999. IL 3–6, RL 5.0

After a cyclone transports her to the Land of Oz, Dorothy must seek out the great wizard to return to Kansas.

Burnett, Frances Hodgson. *The Secret Garden*. New York: Aladdin Classics, 1999. IL 3–6, RL 5.1

Ten-year-old Mary comes to live in a lonely house on the Yorkshire moors and discovers an invalid cousin and the mysteries of a locked garden.

Carroll, Lewis. *Alice's Adventures in Wonderland.* New York: Aladdin Classics, 2000. IL 3–6, RL 5.7

A girl falls down a rabbit hole and discovers a world of nonsensical and amusing characters.

Dumas, Alexandre. *The Three Musketeers.* New York: Puffin Books, 1994, ©1986. IL 5–8, RL 7.3

The heroic young D'Artagnan and his noble compatriots Athos, Porthos, and Aramis are pitted against the master of intrigue, Cardinal Richelieu, and the quintessential wicked woman, Lady de Winter.

George, Jean Craighead. *My Side of the Mountain.* New York: Dutton, 1988. IL 5–8, IL 6.7

A young boy relates his adventures during the year he spends living alone in the Catskill Mountains. He details his struggle for survival, his dependence on nature, his animal friends, and his ultimate realization that he needs human companionship.

Grahame, Kenneth. *The Wind in the Willows.* New York: Puffin Books, 1994, ©1908. IL 5–8, RL 7.4

The escapades of four animal friends who live along a river in the English countryside: Toad, Mole, Rat, and Badger.

London, Jack. *The Call of the Wild.* New York: Puffin Books, 1994, ©1982. IL 5–8, RL 6.0

Buck, who is half St. Bernard and half Scotch shepherd, is abducted and taken to the Klondike, where he reverts to the wild and becomes the leader of a pack of wolves.

Stevenson, Robert Louis. *Kidnapped.* New York: Alfred A. Knopf, 1994. IL 5–8, RL 8.9

After being kidnapped by his villainous uncle, 16-year-old David Balfour escapes and becomes involved in the struggle of the Scottish highlanders against English rule.

Wyss, Johann David. *The Swiss Family Robinson.* New York: Puffin Books, 1994, ©1986. IL 5–8, RL 7.0

Relates the fortunes of a shipwrecked family as they adapt to life on an island with abundant animal and plant life.

Popular Contemporary Literature

Booktalk

Almond, David. *Skellig.* New York: Delacorte Press, 1999. IL 5–8, RL 3.5

Life is changing for Michael, and not necessarily for the better. His parents have just bought a new house. It isn't exactly new, though. In fact, it's a dump. It's going to take a lot of hard work to make it livable. On top of all this, Michael's baby sister is very ill. She is in and out of the hospital, and Michael is afraid she might die. When Michael explores the rundown garage out back, he sees something that he isn't sure is really there. It looks like a man but different. "He was sitting with his legs stretched out and his head tipped back against the wall. He was covered in dust and webs like everything else and his face was thin and pale. Dead bluebottles were scattered on his hair and shoulders." Michael decides to befriend the "man," called Skellig. It turns out Skellig is not quite what he seems. He isn't quite a man, but what is he? And why is he living in this rundown garage? To learn the secret, read *Skellig*.

Learning Extension Ideas

1. This book is rich in descriptive language. Ask students: Who or what do you think Skellig is? Support your ideas with information from the book. Draw a sketch of what you think Skellig is, based on vocabulary from the book and support your picture by listing the vocabulary words you used.

2. Have students write an essay and answer the questions: What lesson did you learn from the story? Who was your favorite character? What did you think of the ending? Would you have written a different ending?

Booktalk

Park, Barbara. *Mick Harte Was Here.* New York: Random House, 1996. IL 3–6, RL 5.5

Mick Harte was here, but now he's gone. He was killed in a bicycle accident. Mick was 12 years, 5 months old when the truck hit him. Mick, who once put a snake in the mailbox to scare the mailman. Mick, who once talked like Elmer Fudd for days on end. Mick, who had a great sense of humor. Mick, who was my wonderful little brother. I'm Mick's sister, Phoebe. I'm 15 years old and I miss Mick a lot. Let me tell you about my brother. I think you'll agree that the world is better off because *Mick Harte Was Here*.

Learning Extension Ideas

1. Discuss eulogies. Ask students: Why are they given? Who usually gives them? Have students write a eulogy for themselves or for someone they love. What do they want to be remembered for?

2. Mick is killed by the truck because he is not wearing his bike helmet. Have the students create posters to promote bicycle safety, including the use of helmets. The posters can be hung throughout the school.

Booktalk

Paulsen, Gary. *Harris and Me.* San Diego: Harcourt Brace, 1993. IL 5–8, RL 5.3

Have you ever known anyone with a drinking problem? Maybe a friend's parent? Maybe someone even closer to you? Well, I'm being raised by two alcoholics. They have trouble enough taking care of themselves, let alone me, so each summer when school lets out, I find myself being farmed out to different relatives just to get me out of their way. This summer I'm off to stay with the Larsons. They have a kid a few years younger than I am, so it might not be too bad. On my first morning on the farm, they wake me up before the sun even comes up! If this is life on the farm, I don't know if it's something I want. Breakfast isn't too bad, but boy, can these farmhands eat! Before the day is out, I get attacked by a rooster and kicked by a cow! I just know this is going to be one interesting summer! And my cousin Harris. What can I say? He is the most rude, vulgar kid I've ever met. He is always trying to get me into trouble. Once again, I find myself the outsider trying to fit in. It can't be any harder than living with my folks, can it?

Learning Extension Ideas

1. In this novel, the parents are described as alcoholics. Have students research alcoholism, then create a flyer that warns about the misuse of alcohol.

2. Have students pretend they are able to enter the novel and create a character for themselves. Students can write a chapter of the book that includes their character. They should be sure to show themselves interacting with others in the novel.

Suggested Further Reading

Blume, Judy. *Just As Long As We're Together.* New York: Bantam Doubleday Dell Books for Young Readers, 1994. IL 5–8, RL 4.7

Stephanie's relationship with her best friend, Rachel, changes during her first year in junior high as she tries to conceal a family problem and meets a new girl from California.

Choldenko, Gennifer. *Notes from a Liar and Her Dog.* New York: Putnam, ©2001. IL 5–8, RL 8.3

Eleven-year-old Ant is stuck in a family she does not like. She copes by pretending that her "real" parents are coming to rescue her, by loving her dog Pistachio, by volunteering at the zoo, and by bending the truth and telling lies.

Cummings, Priscilla. *A Face First.* New York: Dutton Children's Books, ©2001. IL 5–8, RL 6.0

Twelve-year-old Kelley decides to cut off contact with her friends and classmates after suffering third-degree burns to her face and body in a car accident near her home on Maryland's Kent Island.

Deans, Sis Boulos. *Racing the Past.* New York: Henry Holt, 2001. IL 5–8, RL 7.9

After the death of his abusive father, 11-year-old Ricky tries to help his younger brother deal with his residual fears. He also discovers that running helps him deal with his own anger and the taunts of a bullying classmate.

Fleischman, Sid. *Bo & Mzzz Mad.* New York: Greenwillow Books, ©2001. IL 3–6, RL 3.9

When his father dies, Bo Gamage warily moves to the Mojave Desert home of his distant and estranged relatives, the Martinkas. There, he finds that "Mad" lives up to her name, PawPaw despises him, and Aunt Juna hopes he'll help search for the gold mine that started a family feud.

Holt, Kimberly Willis. *Dancing in Cadillac Light.* New York: G. P. Putnam's Sons, ©2001. IL 5–8, RL 6.1

In 1968, 11-year-old Jaynell's life in the town of Moon, Texas, is enlivened when her eccentric Grandpap comes to live with her family.

Horvath, Polly. *Everything on a Waffle.* New York: Farrar, Straus & Giroux, 2001. IL 5–8, RL 5.9

Eleven-year-old Primrose, who lives in a small fishing village in British Columbia, recounts her experiences and all that she learns about human nature and the unpredictability of life in the months after her parents are lost at sea.

Jacques, Brian. *Castaways of the Flying Dutchman.* New York: Philomel, ©2001. IL 5–8, RL 5.1

In 1620, a boy and his dog are rescued from the doomed ship, the *Flying Dutchman,* by an angel who guides them in traveling the world, eternally helping those in great need.

Mikaelsen, Ben. *Touching Spirit Bear.* New York: Harper-Collins, ©2001. IL 5–8, RL 6.7

After his anger erupts into violence, 15-year-old Cole, to avoid going to prison, agrees to participate in a sentencing alternative based on the Native American Circle Justice, and he is sent to a remote Alaskan Island where an encounter with a huge Spirit Bear changes his life.

Zindel, Paul. *The Gadget.* New York: HarperCollins, ©2001. IL 5–8, RL 5.8

In 1945, having joined his father at Los Alamos, where he and other scientists are working on a secret project to end World War II, 13-year-old Stephen becomes caught in a web of secrecy and intrigue.

Adventure and Suspense

Booktalk

Avi. *The True Confessions of Charlotte Doyle.* New York: Orchard Books, 1990. IL 5.8, RL 7.0

My name is Charlotte Doyle and this is my story. I am a refined young woman who was brought up in a proper household. In the year 1832, I set sail aboard the ship *Seahawk* bound from England to Rhode Island. I was the only passenger, and the only female. After we set sail, it became evident that the captain of the ship was not right in the head. In fact, he appeared to be quite mad. Worse yet, the crew was a bunch of lowlifes. They plotted the captain's overthrow. I tried to stay out of it, but that turned out to be impossible. You won't believe what happened to me. I could hardly believe it myself—especially when I was accused of murder! But wait, there's more. Read my story, *The True Confessions of Charlotte Doyle.*

Learning Extension Ideas

1. Have students make a mural showing scenes from the book with captions that explain the pictures. Have small groups illustrate different chapters. Mount the mural around the classroom in the correct chronological order.

2. Charlotte's appearance changed dramatically between the time she boarded the ship and her arrival in America. Have students create two character paper dolls. One should be dressed as the refined Charlotte. The other should be dressed as she appeared at the end of the voyage. Students should include passages from the book to support their characters.

3. Have students research the life and customs of upper-class girls in the first half of the nineteenth century, paying particular attention to how girls were expected to behave. They can then write an instructional booklet that Charlotte's parents may have given her to ensure she retained her manners. Then have them write a booklet of instructions that she could *really* use.

Booktalk

Bodett, Tom. *Williwaw!* New York: Alfred A. Knopf, 2000. IL 5–8, RL 5.9

Ivan lives on a remote piece of land across from Steamer Cove. It is so far from the Alaskan mainland that Ivan and his family don't even have electricity, so of course there's no TV or radio or video games. Ivan relies on his battery-powered game for entertainment. He loves video games. His favorite is *Tech Patrol.* When Ivan's father leaves on an offshore fishing trip, Ivan and his sister talk him into letting them stay on the island by themselves. After his father leaves, Ivan hotwires his video game to the radio and blows them both out. What will they do without a radio? Ivan and September have figured it all out. They can get the chores done and the radio repaired before their father returns. The one thing they didn't count on is the coming williwaw, a fierce northeaster that devastates everything in its path, just like the storm that took the life of their mother. For nonstop action and adventure, read *Williwaw!*

Learning Extension Ideas

1. Williwaws are violent squalls blowing off a mountain, often with hurricane-like winds. Ask students: In what part of the world do they occur? What types of violent storms occur in our area? How do they differ from the williwaw? Write a short story that places

the children in a hurricane instead of a williwaw. How would the events change?

2. Have students create a model or draw a picture of the story's setting. They can use a large box, a piece of cardboard, or a piece of wood and should try to make it as realistic as possible. Make sure they include details important to events in the novel. They can also include the characters. Have them write an accompanying narrative description of their project explaining what it is and its significance.

3. Discuss the role of the story's setting. Students should compare/contrast the setting of this novel with others in which the setting may not be as important.

Booktalk

Durbin, William. *The Broken Blade.* New York: Bantam Books, 1997. IL 3–6, RL 4.8

The year is 1800. Thirteen-year-old Pierre LaPage was supposed to chop the wood for his family, but he didn't. So his father had to do it. But while chopping the wood, Pierre's father had a terrible accident. Now he is unable to take his place as a voyageur with the North West Company. Voyageurs are the men who transport furs by canoe thousands of miles so they can be shipped to Europe. Pierre's family cannot survive without the money his father would have earned on this trip, so Pierre volunteers to take his father's place. Now he must paddle the company's canoe 16 to 18 hours a day with few breaks. He must endure the treacherous waters, and aching, bloodied hands. He also must endure the taunts of the other men on the trip. How will Pierre be able to survive? Find out by joining Pierre on his journey.

Learning Extension Ideas

1. Have students plan a trip with the voyageurs. Tell them to brainstorm a list of all the possible necessities for the canoe trip. Have them write a note to the local trader requesting the needed supplies. They should be sure to include containers to carry the materials and to state a reason why each item was included.

2. Have students create a map that shows Pierre's travels and write annotations for the map to show points of specific interest. They should be sure to follow the story.

Suggested Further Reading

Aiken, Joan. *Dangerous Games.* New York: Delacorte Press, ©1999. IL 5–8, RL 6.7

Her mission to bring an expert on games back to an ailing King James III in London takes Dido Twite to a small tropical island. There she is caught up in the conflict between a conniving city dweller and the more subtle powers of the native forest people.

Avi. *Beyond the Western Sea: Book One: The Escape from Home.* New York: Orchard Books, ©1996. IL 5–8, RL 5.5

Driven from their impoverished Irish village, 15-year-old Maura and her younger brother meet their landlord's runaway son in Liverpool while all three wait for a ship to America.

Hobbs, Will. *Ghost Canoe.* New York: Morrow Junior Books, ©1997. IL 5–8, RL 5.5

Fourteen-year-old Nathan, fishing with the Makah in the Pacific Northwest, finds himself holding a vital clue when a mysterious stranger comes to town looking for Spanish treasure.

Horowitz, Anthony. *The Devil and His Boy.* New York: Philomel Books, 2000. IL 5–8, RL 5.3

In 1593, 13-year-old Tom travels through the English countryside to London, where he falls in with a troupe of actors and finds himself in great danger from several sources.

Karr, Kathleen. *Skullduggery.* New York: Hyperion Books for Children, ©2000. IL 5–8, RL 7.6

In 1839, 12-year-old Matthew's job as assistant to the phrenologist Dr. Cornwall takes him up and down the Eastern Seaboard and to Europe. There they rob graves and try to find out who is following them and why.

Napoli, Donna Jo. *Trouble on the Tracks.* New York: Scholastic, 1997. IL 5–8, RL 4.2

While traveling across the Australian outback on a train, 12-year-old Zach and his younger sister Eve uncover an endangered bird smuggling ring and try to save two trains from a full-speed collision.

Pullman, Philip. *Count Karlstein.* New York: Alfred A. Knopf; distributed by Random House, 1998. IL 5–8, RL 7.1

In the mountains of Switzerland, the wicked Count Karlstein plots to abandon his two nieces in a hunting lodge as prey for the Demon Huntsman and his ghostly hounds.

Schneider, Mical. *Between the Dragon and the Eagle.* Minneapolis, Minn.: Carolrhoda Books, ©1997. IL 5–8, RL 4.5

Courageous adventure-seekers form caravans to transport precious items including a special blue silk along the Silk Road in the year A.D. 100.

Turner, Megan Whalen. *The Thief.* New York: Greenwillow Books, ©1996. IL 5–8, RL 5.5

Gen flaunts his ingenuity as a thief and relishes the adventure that takes him to a remote temple of the gods where he will attempt to steal a precious stone.

Wallace, Barbara Brooks. *Cousins in the Castle.* New York: Atheneum Books for Young Readers, ©1996. IL 5–8, RL 6.0

A new friend comes to Amelia's rescue when she finds herself the victim of a dastardly villain's fiendish plans.

Mystery and Detective Stories

Booktalk

Konigsburg, E. L. *Silent to the Bone.* New York: Atheneum Books for Young Readers, 2000. IL 5–8, RL 6.0

My name is Connor, and my best friend has just stopped talking. It's not that he can't talk; it just seems as if there is something that is not allowing him to talk. Branwell Zamborska has been struck dumb. What could have happened to make Bran stop talking? It all started when he tried to call 911 when his baby sister was hurt. I've been trying to break Bran's silence to find out what happened. How can I possibly do what the doctors can't? Do you think I can help Bran? What do you suppose really happened?

➤ **NOTE:** This book may be too intense for younger students. Teachers are advised to read the book carefully before suggesting it to students.

Learning Extension Ideas

1. A mystery writer must leave clues along the way so that the reader can try to figure out what is going on. Ask students: Can you point to some of the clues in this book and tell how they direct you to the right conclusion?

2. In this book, Connor figures out a way to communicate with Branwell by using index cards with words on them. Ask students: Can you come up with another way to communicate with someone who can't talk? Can you come up with your own language?

Booktalk

Plum-Ucci, Carol. *The Body of Christopher Creed.* San Diego: Harcourt, 2000. IL YA, RL 5.3

Maybe you know someone like Christopher Creed. Everyone knows Christopher; he's the kid in school who is, well, he's a bit weird. He always tags along with other kids even when they don't want him to. He's always got something to say even though no one wants to hear it. And he's always getting beaten up. No one pays too much attention to Christopher until he disappears. Christopher can't even disappear like a regular kid. He sends a note from the school library computer to the principal. It isn't clear from the note whether he plans to run away or to kill himself. Of course, then the rumors start spreading like crazy! In the e-mail, Christopher mentions a few kids that he would like to be. One of the kids is Torey Adams, a seemingly perfect kid who has all the advantages. Now Torey must try to find out what really happened to Christopher. He discovers that Christopher's life was nothing like people thought. Join Torey as he searches for *The Body of Christopher Creed.*

Learning Extension Ideas

1. This novel is especially timely in light of recent events involving school violence. In the book, we are introduced to characters who are reduced to stereotypes based on the cliques they belong to. As Torey gets to know different students, he begins to realize that these stereotypes don't do justice to the teens. In Chris's journal, he describes how he feels about different things that happen to him. Have the students write journal entries describing different characters as Chris would have seen them.

2. Have students examine the stereotypes in the novel. How do they compare to the stereotypes in your school? Do students feel that there is an intense separation among the different cliques? What do they think could be done to bring the cliques together? Should they be? Ask students to write a narrative explaining their responses.

Booktalk

Van Draanen, Wendelin. *Sammy Keyes and the Sisters of Mercy.* New York: Alfred A. Knopf, 1999. IL 5–8, RL 6.0

Sammy got herself into a bit of trouble at school. She's now required to do community service to make up for it. She's supposed to be working at the church to stay out of trouble, not to get into more. Then right in the middle of scrubbing the dirt off the stained glass Baby Jesus, Father Mayhew accuses Sammy of stealing his favorite cross. This looks bad for Sammy because the only people in the church are Father Mayhew and Sammy. So who could it be? Now Sammy is on a quest to find the thief and prove her innocence. When more things come up missing, the case becomes more and more twisted. Who could be stealing? Could it be the homeless girl who comes to the soup kitchen, one of the nuns who run the kitchen, or the visiting merry Sisters of Mercy?

Learning Extension Ideas

1. Have the students brainstorm what makes up a mystery. What are the common elements in a mystery book? Pick out the pieces from the Sammy Keyes book that fit those elements.

2. Have students keep a mystery journal as they read, keeping track of clues and where they think the story is taking them. Have them guess how the story will turn out.

3. Divide the class into groups. Assign each group a character from the book. Have the students describe the character and show examples from the book to support their assessment of the character. They should show how the character is connected to the central character of the book. Ask them: Why is the character important to the story? How would the story change if the character's actions had changed? Have the students discuss the concept of "character" in fiction.

Suggested Further Reading

Benoit, Margaret. *Who Killed Olive Souffle?* New York: Learning Triangle Press, ©1997. IL 5–8, RL 4.2

Detective Angel Cardoni's vacation gets sidetracked when Olive Souffle, the chef at the country inn where Angel is staying, is found dead in the freezer.

Byars, Betsy Cromer. *Dead Letter.* New York: Viking, 1996. IL 5–8, RL 4.8

Herculeah Jones and her best friend Meat set out to crack the case of the mysterious note that she finds in the lining of a secondhand coat.

Dahl, Michael. *The Horizontal Man.* New York: Pocket Books, ©1999. IL 5–8, RL 6.7

Finnegan Zwake investigates the disappearance of an ancient gold, a Mayan figure known as the Horizontal Man.

Hamilton, Virginia. *The House of Dies Drear.* New York: Aladdin Paperbacks, ©1996. IL 5–8, RL 6.0

An African-American family tries to unravel the secrets of their new home, which was once a stop on the Underground Railroad.

Levin, Betty. *Island Bound.* New York: HarperTrophy, 2000, ©1997. IL 5–8, RL 4.8

While trying to prove that he can survive on an island off the coast of Maine, Chris Fossett meets Joellen Roth, who has come to the island with her father to work on a puffin research project. The two become caught up in a mystery surrounding the island's 150-year-old ghost.

Mowry, Jess. *Ghost Train.* New York: Henry Holt, 1996. IL 5–8, RL 5.5

Thirteen-year-old Remi, who has just moved to California from Haiti, and his neighbor Niya, travel back in time to solve the mystery of the night train.

Naylor, Phyllis Reynolds. *The Bomb in the Bessledorf Bus Depot.* New York: Atheneum Books for Young Readers, ©1996. IL 5–8, RL 7.5

After several bombs go off around town, 11-year-old Bernie Magruder becomes suspicious of various members of his family. This causes confusion in Officer Feeney's investigation and around the hotel that Bernie's parents run.

Nixon, Joan Lowery. *Search for the Shadowman.* New York: Delacorte Press, ©1996. IL 5–8, RL 6.5

While working on a genealogy project for his seventh-grade history class, Andy Bonner becomes determined to solve the mystery surrounding a distant relative who was accused of stealing the family fortune.

Raskin, Ellen. *The Westing Game.* New York: Puffin Books, 1997, ©1978. IL 5–8, RL 7.0

The mysterious death of an eccentric millionaire brings together an unlikely assortment of heirs who must uncover the circumstances of his death before they can claim their inheritance.

Roberts, Willo Davis. *Pawns.* New York: Atheneum Books for Young Readers, ©1998. IL 5–8, RL 6.9

After her mother's death and her father's suicide, 14-year-old Teddi finds some stability when she moves in with Mamie, her good-hearted next door neighbor—until the arrival of a woman claiming to be the pregnant wife of Mamie's son who recently died in a plane crash.

Fantasy

Booktalk

Anderson, Janet S. *Going Through the Gate.* New York: Dutton, 1997. IL 3–6

One fine June day, a sixth-grade class is preparing for their graduation ceremony from the county's last one-room school. All the adults in town have gone through this ceremony, but no one will tell the children what is involved. All that is certain is that everyone is changed by "going through the gate." There has never been a problem with the ceremony—except one time 25 years ago. Now the ceremony is about to begin. Find out what it is and what went wrong years ago as the sixth graders prepare for the adventure of *Going Through the Gate.*

Learning Extension Ideas

1. This book is about a rite of passage. Every society has its own rites of passage. Some are religious in nature, some are social. Have students make a list of the things that could be considered a rite of passage. What is the average age for these rites? Some examples are getting a driver's license, getting a part-time job, and being old enough to stay home without a babysitter. Explain how these things can be looked at as rites of passage. Ask students: Can a person experience more than one rite? Write a paragraph about a rite of passage that you are looking forward to.

2. Ask students: Why are rites of passage important? What do they mean to the society? To a child? How do you feel about formal ceremonies to celebrate formal rights of passage? Formal ceremonies include school graduation, religious celebrations, and so forth. Create your own rite of passage and write a proclamation stating the new rite. Explain who is involved, what is celebrated, how it is celebrated, and any other necessary facts.

Booktalk

Levine, Gail Carson. *Ella Enchanted.* New York: Harper-Trophy, 1997. IL 3–6, RL 4.2

Do you long for the day when you will be out from under the thumb of your meddling parents? When you will be free to do what you want instead of what you are told? For Ella, this is really important. You see, Ella is under a spell that requires her to do everything people tell her to do. A misguided fairy gave her a blessing at birth that backfired. The fairy blessed her with obedience. That blessing has turned into a nightmare in which she battles ogres and wicked stepsisters. Does this sound familiar? Well, this version of the Cinderella story has plenty of laughs and unexpected turns. Find out how Ella frees herself from her awful curse.

Learning Extension Ideas

1. Ella's fairy godmother really meant well when she gave Ella the gift of obedience. Have students write a narrative about an incident when they meant to do something good but it turned into something bad. Ask students: How did you feel? How did others treat you? What went wrong?

2. Ask students: If you had a fairy godmother and she could grant you one wish, what would it be? Write a paper on this explaining your wish as thoroughly as possible. The wishes will be presented to the class. Have students try to turn their wishes into curses. It may be easier than people think!

Booktalk

Pullman, Philip. *The Golden Compass.* New York: Alfred A. Knopf, 1995. IL 5–8, RL 6.7

My name is Lyra Belacqua, and this is my daemon Pantalaimon. [You could use a stuffed animal for this.] Don't be afraid of Pantalaimon. Our world is just a bit different from yours. The daemon is what you might call your conscious or your soul. You can't see yours, but you know it's there. I live in England. Oh, not the England you know. You see, although our world is very similar to yours, there are big differences. I am an orphan and I am living at Jordan College. My uncle is a scholar at the school. It is rumored that he has photographed the mysterious "dust." For some reason, that has made him very unpopular. Someone has even tried to kill him. Now he has been taken hostage up North and the mean Mrs. Coulter has evil plans for me. Also, children have been turning up missing. I just know Mrs. Coulter has something to do with it. I must now do something that I never would have imagined. I must sail North with the gyptians to try to save my uncle and to find the lost children. Oh Pantalaimon, what awaits us in the North? And what of this mysterious dust? If you want to find out, you can read about my adventures in *The Golden Compass.*

Learning Extension Ideas

1. In this novel, Lyra lives in a world that is like ours but not like ours. There are some things that are familiar to us, but there are others that are foreign. Ask students: Do you think that there are such things as parallel worlds? Have students describe some of the things they may find in a parallel world.

2. Each of the characters in the book has a daemon that represents his or her soul. These daemons reflect the character of those to whom they belong. Have students choose their own daemons and tell how they reflect their character.

Suggested Further Reading

Alexander, Lloyd. *The Book of Three.* New York: Henry Holt, 1999. IL 5–8, RL 4.8

Taran, Assistant Pig-Keeper to a famous oracular sow, sets out on a hazardous mission to save Prydain from the forces of evil.

Barron, T. A. *The Fires of Merlin.* New York: Philomel Books, ©1998. IL 5–8, RL 6.0

Having voyaged to the Otherworld in his quest to find himself, the young wizard Merlin must face fire in many different forms and deal with the possibility of losing his own magical power.

Billingsley, Franny. *The Folk Keeper.* New York: Atheneum Books for Young Readers, ©1999. IL 5–8, RL 6.0

Orphan Corinna disguises herself as a boy to pose as a Folk Keeper, one who keeps the Evil Folk at bay. She discovers her heritage as a seal maiden when she is taken to live with a wealthy family in their manor by the sea.

Jacques, Brian. *Redwall.* New York: Ace Books, 1998. IL 5–8, RL 7.8

The peaceful life of ancient Redwall Abbey is shattered by the arrival of the evil rat Cluny and his villainous hordes. Matthias, a young mouse, is determined to find the legendary sword of Martin the Warrior that, he is convinced, will help Redwall's inhabitants destroy the enemy.

Lee, Tanith. *Islands in the Sky.* New York: Random House, ©1999. IL 5–8, RL 6.1

While climbing a tree to rescue a kite, 11-year-old Hope is pulled into the sky, away from the reality of life in London in 1867, and into a world of magic.

O'Shea, Pat. *The Hounds of the Morrigan.* New York: HarperTrophy, 1999. IL 5–8, RL 6.9

When a 10-year-old boy finds an old book of magic in a bookshop in Ireland, the forces of good and evil gather to do battle over the book.

Pattou, Edith. *Fire Arrow: The Second Song of Eirren.* San Diego: Harcourt Brace, ©1998. IL 5–8, RL 7.3

While on the trail of her father's murderers, the young archer Brie discovers her birthright—a magical arrow—and the sinister doings of an evil sorcerer.

Pierce, Tamora. *Magic Steps.* New York: Scholastic, 2000. IL 5–8, RL 6.8

When drawn into the investigation of murders perpetrated on a powerful family in Summersea, Sandry and her student Pasco undertake the dangerous mission of entrapping the invisible killers.

Rowling, J. K. *Harry Potter and the Sorcerer's Stone.* New York: A. A. Levine Books, 1998. IL 5–8, RL 5.3

Rescued from the outrageous neglect of his aunt and uncle, a young boy with a great destiny proves his worth while attending Hogwarts School of Witchcraft and Wizardry.

Turner, Megan Whalen. *The Queen of Attolia.* New York: Greenwillow Books, ©2000. IL 5–8, RL 5.6

Forsaken by the gods and left to his own devices, Eugenides, Royal Thief of Eddis, summons all his wits and wiles in an attempt to conquer the rival Queen of Attolia.

6 ⚬ Mathematics

Introduction

Mathematics is much more than arithmetic and geometry. It involves measurement, inference, deduction, and more. Mathematics is directly applicable to the physical and biological sciences as well as computer science. Using mathematics to find patterns and statistical analysis is directly applicable to history.

When teaching mathematical concepts to children, it is sometimes easier to use picture books. Picture books that appeal to early elementary students often deal with concepts being taught or reinforced in the older grades. Children respond to the simple stories while getting practice with the concepts being taught. There are also some novels geared to older children that help in the teaching of mathematics. Using literature that deals directly or indirectly with mathematical concepts makes these concepts more accessible to many children. Students who enjoy the story or the characters are more apt to want to figure out the problems. Stories help enliven and make math concepts real. Using stories is helpful when reviewing specific mathematical principles and tasks. Through the stories, students are more apt to learn the principles.

This chapter looks at books that can be used to support the study of mathematics. Although many are grade level materials, the use of picture books to explain concepts is especially appropriate to mathematics. For that reason, several early elementary level books are included here.

Booktalk

Burns Marilyn; illustrated by Debbie Tilley. *Spaghetti and Meatballs for All!: A Mathematical Story.* New York: Scholastic, 1997. IL K–3, RL 3.5

Mr. and Mrs. Comfort are enjoying a beautiful summer day. Mrs. Comfort works on her garden while Mr. Comfort reads a cookbook. Then Mrs. Comfort comes up with a wonderful idea. They decide to have a family reunion! They carefully plan the menu and the seating arrangements to be sure that everyone will have

---

RL = Reading Level   *IL = Interest Level*

enough. As the guests begin to arrive, chaos breaks out. The guests rearrange the tables. Mrs. Comfort is worried that there will not be enough room for everyone. Is she right? How will this situation work out? Will there be enough *Spaghetti and Meatballs for All?*

Learning Extension Ideas

1. Mr. Comfort loved reading cookbooks in the garden. Using recipes from different cookbooks, have the students modify a recipe to feed the guests at the Comfort's party.

2. Using graph paper, have the students work in groups to draw the different configurations of the tables as the story is being read. Alternately, use manipulatives to arrange the tables. How many guests could be seated in each variation?

Booktalk

Enzensberger, Hans Magnus. *The Number Devil: A Mathematical Adventure.* New York: Metropolitan Books, 1998. IL YA, RL 7.0

Have you ever had a bad dream? Well, Robert has bad dreams every night. He hates having these bad dreams. Once he dreamed a big ugly fish was swallowing him. He dreamed he was sliding down an endless slide going faster and faster and couldn't stop. Boy, does he hate these dreams! Then he comes up with a way to stop them. He will simply not give into them. But now that he has gotten rid of the fish and the slide, he is confronted by a new dream. In this dream, the number devil comes to him each night. What do they talk about? Mathematics! The number devil explains math to Robert, who is not really all that interested. Each night, the math problems become more and more complex. Poor Robert! Will he ever be able to get a good night's sleep? Or will he be forever haunted by *The Number Devil?*

Learning Extension Ideas

1. Have students write short stories or picture books for younger children that include some math facts. They may use examples from *The Number Devil.*

2. Have students write about one of the chapters that they learned from. Ask them: Why do you think the number devil's explanation made more sense than the textbook? Could you explain the concept to someone else now?

Booktalk

Lasky, Kathryn; illustrated by Kevin Hawkes. *The Librarian Who Measured the Earth.* Boston: Little, Brown, 1994. IL 3–6, RL 5.7

Over 2,000 years ago, a young boy was born in what is now known as Libya. The young boy was named Eratosthenes. He was no ordinary boy. You see, Eratosthenes was a very curious young man and he asked questions wherever he went. Although he was a good student in every subject, his favorite subject was geography. He often wondered how big the earth was. Two thousand years ago, no one had yet ventured out into the oceans to see what was beyond the horizon. It was a well-known fact by Eratosthenes's time that the earth was round, but no one could tell how big it was. Eratosthenes's life took a new direction when he was called to the great city of Alexandria to be teacher to King Ptolemy's son. This was the home of the most brilliant men of the time and also home to the world's greatest library. Eratosthenes became one of the librarians. He was able to use the library for his research. He kept coming back to his primary question: Just how big is the world? After many tries, Eratosthenes found the answer. How did he do it?

Learning Extension Ideas

1. Have students visit the Mathgoodies Web site at http://www.mathgoodies.com and choose an activity about circumference.

2. Several other mathematicians are mentioned in the book. Have students research their contributions. Reports can be written on scrolls (e.g., 8½-by-14-inch pieces of paper used horizontally and rolled for storage). The scrolls can be kept in tubes to replicate the storage of materials in the great library of Alexandria. Potato chip canisters make good holders.

Booktalk

Manes, Stephen; illustrated by George Ulrich. *Make Four Million Dollar$ by Next Thur$day.* New York: Bantam Skylark, 1991. IL 3–6, RL 5.3

Jason is desperate for money. He's lost his allowance and doesn't have any idea where it might be. He borrows his brother's metal detector to go back to the park to try to locate his missing money. He doesn't find the allowance, but he does find a copy of Dr. Silverfish's new book, *Make Four Million Dollar$ by Next Thur$day.* Could it be for real? Could this possibly work? Well, Jason is determined to find out. He needs to follow the directions in the book precisely, which puts him into some pretty embarrassing spots. How far will Jason go to get rich? Follow his humorous exploits as he tries to *Make Four Million Dollar$ by Next Thur$Day!*

Learning Extension Ideas

1. Have students search newspapers, magazines, and television advertisements for examples of "get rich quick" schemes. Ask students: Do you think any of them might work? How do you think they accomplish what they say they will?

2. In this book, Jason does some pretty outlandish things in the belief that they will help him get rich. Ask students: How far would you go to get rich? What would you be willing to do? How much would you be willing to spend? Would you spend $1 to make $100?

3. Ask students: If you were successful in your pursuit, what would you do with the money? How would you spend the $4 million? Or would you spend it? Invest it? Save it? Make a list of expenditures, investments, and savings and put them into a chart.

Booktalk

Sachar, Louis. *Holes.* New York: Farrar, Straus & Giroux, 1998. IL YA, RL 6.5

Stanley was having a bad day—a very bad day. He was assaulted by the class bully in the boy's room and his notebook was thrown into the toilet. Now he is walking home with a very soggy notebook. Could things get any worse? Suddenly, from out of the blue, he is hit on the head by a very smelly pair of baseball shoes! These shoes are huge and Stanley has never smelled anything quite this bad! Turns out these shoes belonged to no other than Clyde "Sweet Feet" Livingston. Unfortunately, these same shoes have just been stolen from a charity. How can Stanley expect anyone to believe that he didn't steal them—they just fell out of the sky? Well, he can't. Stanley is found guilty and given a choice of spending time in jail or going to Camp Green Lake. Since he had never been to camp before, he chose Camp Green Lake. Unfortunately, life at "camp" convinced Stanley that there really was something to the family curse that he heard so much about. You see, it all went back to his no-good-dirty-rotten-pig-stealing-great-great-grandfather. Each day, the boys at Camp Green Lake are required to dig a hole in the desert. Not just a little hole. No, the boys had to dig a hole five feet deep and five feet wide. That's no easy task. Especially for someone like Stanley, who is not in the best physical shape. Now his life will be spent digging holes in the desert. Can Stanley survive? Join Stanley as he digs *Holes*.

Learning Extension Ideas

1. Have students measure out in the classroom how large five feet by five feet is. Then give the students graph paper and have them draw the classroom to scale (e.g., one square = one foot). Have them draw the holes on the graph paper. Ask them: How many holes will fit on the graph paper? How does this relate to how many would fit into the classroom? Have the students discuss scale in relation to the holes they have drawn. How is it similar to scales used on maps?

2. Have the students calculate the area of the hole.

3. The name Stanley Yelnats is a palindrome. Have students create as many palindromes as they can think of in a specified amount of time and then share them with the class. Keep track of the answers. Have students make a bar graph of how many were made with three letters, four letters, and so forth. Find the mean, median, and mode length of the words.

Booktalk

Sachar, Louis. *Sideways Arithmetic from Wayside School.* New York: Scholastic, 1989. IL 3–6, RL 5.1

Sue just finished reading a book about the Wayside School and has decided that she wants to attend. That is not too uncommon. Many students decide to go to Wayside School after reading about it because they think that all the kids do is eat ice cream, draw pictures, and watch movies about turtles. Not too hard to take, right? Well, Sue is in for a big surprise in Mrs. Jewls's class. When it's time for math, she tells to kids to take out their spelling books! Now why on earth would they need their spelling books in math class? The first math problem they are given is to add elf+elf. What?? Sue is totally confused. How can you add elf+elf? When one of the students comes up with the answer— fool—Sue begins to think there is something terribly wrong with this school! Join Sue as she learns how to do *Sideways Arithmetic from Wayside School.*

Learning Extension Ideas

1. You may want to read this book aloud to your students. Put the problems on the board and have the students try to solve them. Give them the hints that are in the book. How many can they solve?

2. Have the students come up with their own sideways arithmetic problems. Collect them in a notebook and ask others to try to solve them. Be sure to have the students provide an answer key to their problems!

Booktalk

Scieszka, Jon, and Lane Smith. *Math Curse.* New York: Viking, 1995. IL K–3, RL 3.0

Was there ever a time when someone made a suggestion and you just couldn't stop thinking about it? Maybe they asked if you were hungry and you really weren't until they mentioned it. But now all you can think of is how hungry you are. Well, in this book, a young girl falls under a math curse! First, her teacher, Mrs. Fibonacci, tells the class that you can think of almost everything as a math problem. That was on Monday. By Tuesday the curse is in full force. The girl starts thinking of everything as a math problem! If it takes 10 minutes to get dressed, 15 minutes to eat breakfast, and 1 minute to brush your teeth, and your bus leaves at 8:00, when do you have to start getting ready? All day long, everything turns into a math problem. It can't be stopped! Can you come up with the solutions to help her? Will her life ever be the same? Will yours? Or will you fall under the spell of the *Math Curse?*

Learning Extension Ideas

1. Ask the students to discuss the idea that almost everything can be a math problem. Have them brainstorm other math problems from the world around them and write their own questions.

2. Students can create their own "Math Curse" book filled with examples from their own lives. Divide them into groups and have each group come up with one page of the story. They will need to create the word problem and illustrate the page. The completed book can be bound and added to the classroom collection.

Booktalk

Tompert, Ann. *Grandfather Tang's Story.* New York: Crown, ©1990. IL K–3, RL 3.6

Little Soo begs Grandfather Tang to tell her a story. Using shapes created by tangrams, Grandfather tells her the tale of two magical foxes, Wu Ling and Chou. These two friends can change shape in the wink of an eye. They change into a variety of animals such as a wolf and a bird. How do they do it? With tangrams. Join Little Soo as she listens to *Grandfather Tang's Story* and learn about tangrams.

Learning Extension Ideas

1. Grandfather Tang uses tangrams to tell his granddaughter a story. Read this story to students using an overhead projector with the tangrams on top. Have students arrange the tangrams on the overhead to create the different animals.

2. Students can use the tangrams to create their own animals. Have them work in pairs to come up with other animals. The children can put these on the overhead and have others try to guess what the animal is.

Suggested Further Reading

Anno, Masaichiro. *Anno's Mysterious Multiplying Jar.* New York: Philomel, 1983. IL 5–8, RL 6.0

Simple text and pictures introduce the mathematical concept of factorials.

Bauer, Joan. *Sticks.* New York: Bantam Doubleday Dell Books for Young Readers, 1997. IL 3–6, RL 6.0

With the help of his grandmother, his dead father's best friend, and his own best friend (a math genius), 10-year-old Mickey prepares to compete in the most important pool championship of his life, despite his mother's reservations.

Burns, Marilyn. *The Greedy Triangle.* New York: Scholastic, ©1994. IL K–3, RL 4.7

Dissatisfied with its shape, a triangle keeps asking the local shapeshifter to add more lines and angles until it doesn't know which side is up.

Isdell, Wendy. *A Gebra Named Al: A Novel.* Minneapolis, Minn.: Free Spirit, ©1993. IL YA, RL 7.0

Trouble with her algebra homework leads Julie through a mysterious portal into the Land of Mathematics, where a zebra-like Imaginary Number and creatures representing Periodic Elements help her learn about math and chemistry in order to get home.

Juster, Norton. *The Dot & The Line: A Romance in Lower Mathematics.* New York: SeaStar Books, 2001. IL YA, RL 7.0

A mathematical fable in which a line's love for a dot urges him to new heights of expression, winning her away from the chaotic squiggle. Shows the many applications of lines in drawings and in daily life.

Lumpkin, Beatrice. *Senefer: A Young Genius in Old Eygpt i.e., Egypt.* Trenton, N.J.: Africa World Press, 1992. IL 3–6, RL 5.5

Teaches young readers that mathematics can be fun by telling the story of Senefer, an African child in ancient Egypt who became a famous mathematician and engineer.

Pittman, Helena Clare. *A Grain of Rice.* New York: Bantam Doubleday Dell Books for Young Readers, 1996, ©1986. IL K–3, RL 4.1

A clever, cheerful, hard-working farmer's son wins the hand of a Chinese princess by outwitting her father, the emperor, who treasures his daughter more than all the rice in China.

Rockwell, Thomas. *How to Get Fabulously Rich.* New York: Franklin Watts, 1990. IL 5–8, RL 6.1

After Billy wins $410,000 in the lottery, his friends claim that he owes them a share for helping him play, creating a tangle of lies, memory, and money.

Schwartz, David M. *If You Made a Million.* New York: Lothrop, Lee & Shepard, ©1989. IL K–3, RL 3.9

Describes the various forms that money can take, including coins, paper money, and personal checks, and how it can be used to make purchases, pay off loans, or build interest in the bank.

Tahan, Malba. *The Man Who Counted: A Collection of Mathematical Adventures.* New York: Norton, 1993. IL YA

Adventures of Beremiz Samir, who uses his extraordinary mathematical skills to settle disputes, give advice, overcome enemies, and win fame and fortune.

7  Science

Introduction

The study of science is important to all students. During the middle school grades, they study earth and space science. This includes the understanding of atmospheric processes and the water cycle. Middle schoolers study weather phenomena and what weather patterns mean to humans. They also study Earth's composition and structure, as well as the composition and structure of the universe and Earth's place in it. In life science, students learn the principles of heredity and related concepts. The also study the structure and function of cells and organisms and the relationships among organisms and their physical environment. Biological evolution and the diversity of life is a part of the curriculum in the middle years. Students also are introduced to physical science, which involves the study of heat, light, electricity, magnetism, and energy. By understanding these concepts, students can begin to understand the universe and our place in it. Finally, the study of scientific inquiry is explored. How do scientists know what they know? To answer fundamental questions, scientists must be able to explore concepts and make predictions. Science inquiry includes the understanding of the nature of scientific knowledge, the nature of scientific inquiry, and the scientific enterprise.

Using literature to help the students with these concepts is a natural. The stories of science breathe life into a subject that is too often perceived as difficult or dry. And with literature, learning goes beyond rote memorization to deeper understanding of concepts and ideas. The following books often stimulate readers to further explore science issues. This chapter explores literature that touches on these four themes of science.

RL = Reading Level   *IL = Interest Level*

Earth and Space Sciences

Booktalk

Armstrong, Jennifer. *Shipwreck at the Bottom of the World: The Extraordinary True Story of Shackleton and the Endurance.* New York: Crown, 1998. IL 5–8, RL 6.5 (Nonfiction)

During the winter, the temperature here can get down to 100 degrees below zero F. Winds can top 200 miles per hour. The seas around the land begin to freeze at a rate of two miles every minute until the frozen area around the continent is larger than the entire United States. It is the only continent in the world that is totally covered in ice and snow. This is the most hostile environment on Earth. It's the Antarctic.

In August 1914, Ernest Shackleton and his crew left England in an attempt to be the first explorers to cross Antarctica from one end to the other. They set off with great hope, never suspecting what hardships awaited them. Months later, still miles from land, the ship became icebound. The ship could not move and the crew was forced to spend the winter in the cruel Antarctic winter. Then the ice began to break, but it crushed the ship. There was only one hope. A small group of men set off to find help. This incredible true story is told in the words of the survivors and has photographs taken by the men in the crew. Join Captain Shackleton and his men as they endure the *Shipwreck at the Bottom of the World.*

Learning Extension Ideas

1. Ernest Shackleton showed what a true leader can accomplish. He kept the men going when there seemed to be no hope. Have the students brainstorm the qualities of leadership and explain how Shackleton demonstrated these qualities. Ask them: Would these same qualities be needed if the men were stranded in a different environment?

2. Have the students plan a trip to Antarctica. What equipment would they need? What kind of food supplies? Have them chart out a course on a world trip and determine how long it would take to reach their destination. Then they can prepare a list of gear needed to endure the weather conditions.

3. Have students visit the following Web sites to view the amazing photographs from the expedition and learn more about that legendary trip.

   • *The Endurance: Shackleton's Legendary Antarctic Expedition,* http://www.amnh.org/exhibitions/shackleton/index.html

- *Shackleton's Antarctic Odyssey*, http://www.pbs.org/wgbh/nova
  /shackleton. At this site, PBS Nova Online Adventure offers classroom resources, such as lesson plans, iceberg analysis data,
  astronomy, nutrition, and further Internet links.

Booktalk

Duey, Kathleen. *Hurricane: Open Seas, 1844.* New York: Aladdin, 1999. IL 3–6, RL 3.8

Imagine living on a boat, at sea for years at a time. It's been four long years
since Rebecca Whittier has seen her friends in New Bedford. Her father is
the captain of the whaler *Vigilance*, and the family has been at sea for a long
time. Rebecca hopes that they find enough whales soon, so she can return
home. Life aboard a whaling ship in 1844 is not easy. The food is full of bugs,
the crew is unruly, and Rebecca is forced to stay below decks most of the
time. Her younger brother is not restricted and is allowed to help the men.
When the men catch two whales in one day, Rebecca hopes that their journey
may be coming to an end. As she and her mother bake a special treat of donuts
for the men to celebrate, a strong wind picks up. As the night approaches, the
wind gets stronger. Soon they are heading into the heart of a hurricane. Rebecca
finds herself fighting for survival alongside a young indentured servant.

Learning Extension Ideas

1. Obviously there was no way to predict hurricanes in Rebecca's
   time. Ask students: How do weather forecasters today know when
   hurricanes will strike? Are they always right?

2. Have students pretend they are the mayor of a small town in
   Florida. The weather service has predicted that a hurricane may
   hit the town. What further information would they need to decide
   whether to order an evacuation of the town?

3. Have students track hurricanes during the hurricane season. Keep
   track also of the amount of damage caused by each storm. Were
   there any strange occurrences during the season?

4. Ask students: What precautions should people take during a hurricane watch? During a hurricane warning? Create an informational
   press release that will tell people what they should do in case of
   emergency.

Booktalk

Krakauer, Jon. *Into Thin Air.* New York: Villard Books, 1997. IL AD (Nonfiction)

In the spring of 1996, a reporter started out on the journey of a lifetime. On assignment for *Outside Magazine*, Jon Krakauer started on his quest to climb the highest mountain in the world, Mt. Everest. Jon joined Rob Hall, an experienced guide who had successfully led several expeditions to the summit of the mountain. Things started out just as planned. Krakauer interviewed the other climbers to get their feelings about this incredible journey. The cost of climbing the mountain was high, and it took a great deal of money as well as courage to take on the climb. Krakauer introduces the reader to several different people who have the same goal in mind, to make it to the summit. Some are repeat climbers who had not reached the summit before. As the climb goes forward, Krakauer begins to fear that things may not go well. Then there are some accidents, and some suspicious decisions are made. Little did the climbers know that spring 1996 would bring some of the most deadly weather in Everest history. Join Jon Krakauer and the rest of the climbers as they ascend *Into Thin Air.*

> ➤ **NOTE:** This book may be too intense for younger students. Teachers are advised to read the book carefully before suggesting it to students. Although written for adults, middle school students are drawn to the story and enjoy reading about this expedition.

Learning Extension Ideas

1. Have students create a travel brochure for Rob Hall and the expedition. What information would they stress? Would it be illustrated? With what images? What environmental conditions would they highlight?

2. Divide students into groups. Assign one chapter to each group. Each will be responsible for creating a PowerPoint presentation for its chapter. The groups should include illustrations. Have students give their PowerPoint presentations in chronological order as they retell the story of Jon Krakauer's experience on Mt. Everest. They should highlight the shifting weather patterns and how the weather affected the abilities of the climbers to think and maneuver.

Booktalk

Murphy, Jim. *Blizzard: The Storm That Changed America.* New York: Scholastic, 2000. IL 5–8, RL 5.9 (Nonfiction)

That day did not seem to be any different than those that had come before. There was nothing that hinted of what was to come. But on March 12, 1888, the skies along the East Coast of the United States turned an ugly gray and a horrible thing happened. The storm of the century hit. At that time, there were no television weather forecasters to warn that they were in for the storm of the century. There were no Doppler radar or Accuweather reports. Just lots of snow. More snow than anyone could possibly have imagined. And it wasn't the kind of snow that is fun to play in; it was a heavy snow that came so fast people became immobilized. Some became trapped in the fast falling snow and froze while trying to walk home. They knew that they must keep walking so they wouldn't freeze, but the snow became too deep to get through. By the end of the storm 36 hours later, more than 50 inches of snow had fallen, with drifts up to 50 feet high. How could people function? How could the snow be cleaned up? This is a true story told in the words of some of the survivors of this incredible storm. Read the story of one of the worst snowstorms in U.S history in *Blizzard*.

Learning Extension Ideas

1. The storm raged for days while people along the East Coast battled for survival. Have students create a timeline of the storm. They should be sure to include snow accumulation as the storm progressed.

2. Snowstorms are common in the Northeast. Ask students what types of severe weather are more common in other parts of the country. Have them use a map of the United States to indicate where storms occur. They can use symbols to indicate tornadoes, hurricanes, blizzards, williwaws, and so forth.

3. Ask students how they would survive a severe storm. What types of precautions can be taken to ensure safety? Have them compile a list of items to be placed in a survival kit.

4. Ask students: In what ways did the Blizzard of 1888 change the people who lived through it?

Booktalk

Ruckman, Ivy. *Night of the Twisters.* New York: Harper-Trophy, 1986. IL 5–8, RL 4.8

It started out as just an ordinary day for Dan Hatch and his friend Arthur. Dreaming of summer vacation, they lay on their backs watching the clouds roll by. Nothing told them that this day would change their lives forever. By the time the boys rode their bicycles to Dan's house, the clouds were black and the wind was whipping. Dan was sure there was a storm on the way. But even Dan had no idea how bad it would get. Join Dan, Arthur, and Dan's baby brother as they face the *Night of the Twisters.*

Learning Extension Ideas

1. Ask students: What was the area like where the boys lived? Why didn't they think the tornado would hit their area?

2. Ask students: What causes tornadoes; when and where are they most likely to hit? In what direction do they travel?

3. Ask students: What can we do to prepare for a tornado, and what should we do if one hits? What items should we have on hand to prepare for a large storm?

4. Ask students: What are the various agencies that come to help when this type of disaster happens, and what are their jobs?

5. Ask students: How can we prepare for an earthquake, and what should we do if one occurs?

6. Have students create their own tornado in a jar using the following instructions.

MATERIALS NEEDED

8 oz. jar with lid	Clear liquid dish soap
Water	Glitter
Vinegar	

MAKE IT HAPPEN

1. Fill the jar three-quarters full with water.

2. Put in one teaspoon of vinegar and one teaspoon of dish soap.

3. Sprinkle in a small amount of glitter.

4. Close the lid and rotate the jar to see a tornado form.

Suggested Further Reading

Campbell, Eric. *The Shark Callers.* San Diego: Harcourt Brace, 1994. IL YA, RL 5.5

Two teenage boys, one on a shark hunt and the other traveling with his family, face the challenge of their lives when a volcano erupts, causing a massive tidal wave in the South Seas.

Duey, Kathleen. *Blizzard, Estes Park, Colorado, 1886.* New York: Aladdin, 1998. IL 3–6, RL 5.2

When 12-year-old Maggie attempts to rescue Hadyn during a sudden blizzard in the Colorado mountains in 1886, both cousins change their minds about each other.

Garland, Sherry. *The Silent Storm.* San Diego: Harcourt Brace, 1995. IL 5–8, RL 5.5

Thirteen-year-old Alyssa has not spoken since seeing her parents die in a hurricane. Now, three years later, another storm threatens the home she shares with her grandfather on Galveston Island.

Gregory, Kristiana. *Earthquake at Dawn.* San Diego: Harcourt Brace, ©1992. IL 5–8, RL 6.3

A novelization of 22-two-year-old photographer Edith Irvine's experiences in the aftermath of the 1906 San Francisco Earthquake, as seen through the eyes of 15-year-old Daisy, a fictitious traveling companion.

Hamilton, Virginia. *Drylongso.* San Diego: Harcourt Brace, 1997, ©1992. IL 5–8, RL 4.6

As a great wall of dust moves across their drought-stricken farm, a family's distress is relieved by a young man called Drylongso, who literally blows into their lives with the storm.

Jones, Martha Tannery. *Terror from the Gulf: A Hurricane in Galveston.* Dallas, Tex.: Hendrick-Long, ©1999. IL 5–8, RL 7.0

In 1900 in Galveston, Texas, 12-year-old Charlie, who fears the sea because of a boating accident that killed his father, overcomes his personal demons to survive a terrible hurricane.

Kehret, Peg. *Earthquake Terror.* New York: Cobblehill Books, ©1996. IL 5–8, RL 4.2

When an earthquake hits the isolated island in northern California where his family was camping, 12-year-old Jonathan Palmer must find a way to keep himself, his partially paralyzed younger sister, and their dog alive until help arrives.

Lauber, Patricia. *Flood: Wrestling with the Mississippi.* Washington, D.C.; Emeryville, Calif.: National Geographic Society; distributed by Publishers Group West, ©1996. IL 5–8, RL 5.5

Describes the history of flooding of the Mississippi River, focusing on the 1927 and 1993 floods, the effects on people near the river, and efforts to prevent flooding.

Ruckman, Ivy. *No Way Out.* New York: HarperKeypoint, 1989. IL YA, RL 6.7

Hiking along the Virgin River in Utah, 19-year-old Amy, her brother, and five friends battle a flash flood.

Smith, Roland. *Sasquatch.* New York: Hyperion Paperbacks for Children, 1999, ©1998. IL 5–8, RL 5.2

In an attempt to protect the resident Sasquatch from ruthless hunters, 13-year-old Dylan follows his father into the woods on the slopes of Mount St. Helens, which is on the brink of another eruption.

Life Science

Booktalk

Anderson, Laurie Halse. *Fever 1793.* New York: Simon & Schuster Books for Young Readers, 2000. IL YA, RL 4.4

Fourteen-year-old Mattie Cook has a pretty good life in Philadelphia. The year is 1793, and Mattie has great plans for her future in spite of the fact that her mother is determined to marry her off to some awful son of a wealthy family. What Mattie wants to do is to turn the Cook Coffeehouse into the finest business in Philadelphia. After all, her mother has been running the business by herself ever since Mattie's father died. And there is no reason why Mattie can't run the business herself. She can read and write and do her figures, too. She might even expand the business into the lot next door.

It is August and the heat is oppressive. Rumors start buzzing as annoyingly as the never-ceasing mosquitoes: rumors of fever. At first, people are not too worried. Just a summer fever, nothing serious. But as more and more people fall ill, panic sets in. Those who are able escape from the city. Others shut themselves in their houses and don't venture outside. Suddenly, Mattie finds herself in a situation she could never have prepared for. She has contracted yellow fever! Trapped in a living nightmare, she must do all she can to stay alive. What is life like during an outbreak of a contagious disease? What can people in 1793 do to help those stricken? What will happen to Mattie?

Learning Extension Ideas

1. It wasn't until 1902 that the cause of yellow fever was discovered. Dr. Walter Reed discovered that the disease was spread by mosquitoes. Ask students: What other illnesses devastated populations that have now been cured? Have students research and report on diseases of the past.

2. The West Nile virus was recently identified as being carried by mosquitoes. Have students find and read news stories about the virus. Ask them: How have the media portrayed the illness? Do you feel the news agencies have exaggerated the danger or just warned the public? What images have been shown to accompany the articles? How do they affect the story? What is the role of the media in disseminating information about this virus?

Booktalk

DeFelice, Cynthia. *The Apprenticeship of Lucas Whitaker.* New York: Farrar, Straus & Giroux, 1996. IL 5–8, RL 5.5

Eleven-year-old Lucas is doing the best he can to care for his mother. After watching the rest of his family die, he is certain that his mother will follow. Like the rest of the family, she has consumption. This is what people in the 1840s called the disease tuberculosis. Lucas thought that there was no cure and no real treatment. He did what he could, but he couldn't save his mother. After he has buried her, a neighbor comes by to tell him of a cure that had worked with his son, but it is too late for Lucas's mother. Now Lucas feels he must leave his home and neighbors and get away from the pain he feels over the loss of his family. He runs for several days. He ends up in a town south of his home. There he finds work as an apprentice to the town doctor. From the doctor, he learns about helping sick people. The town is also suffering from an outbreak of consumption. The doctor tells them there is no cure, but the townsfolk have heard of the mystery cure—the same cure that Lucas had been told of by his neighbor. Can the "cure" really work? Is it science or superstition? Join Lucas as he learns the difference between science and superstition.

Learning Extension Ideas

1. When illness breaks out and there is no known cure, it is not uncommon for desperate people to grasp at any claim or miracle cure. Ask students: Can you think of some "cures" that are being touted today? What illnesses are they supposed to cure?

2. Ask students: Does tuberculosis still exist today, or has it been wiped out? Research the progression of treatments used for tuberculosis.

Booktalk

Mowat, Farley. *Lost in the Barrens.* New York: Bantam, 1984. IL YA, RL 6.4

Awasin and Jamie are neighbors from very different backgrounds. Jamie was put in boarding school after his parents died, until his trapper uncle could no longer afford the expense. Awasin is the son of the leader of the Cree camp that Jamie and his uncle lived near. When the adults are off on a trip to sell their trappings, the camp is approached by a group of Chipeweyans looking for ammunition to continue their search for their life source, the deer. Awasin decides to personally deliver the loan to be sure the group is not lying. After seeing starving people, Awasin mistakenly signs the boys up for the full trip in search of the deer. Awasin and Jamie were looking for adventure. Now they have one—from running rapids to surviving in arctic conditions, constructing shelter, and hiding their food from wolverines. Through their experiences they learn to respect each other and deal with their fears.

Learning Extension Ideas

1. Ask students: What is hypothermia? What are the symptoms? Create a poster to explain how the human body regulates its temperature. Explain how cold weather affects the body and what the effects of hypothermia are.

2. Ask students: How do you think the boys were feeling during their adventures? Have students pick one of the young men and write a letter home explaining what they are going through and how they feel about it.

Booktalk

Park, Barbara. *The Graduation of Jake Moon.* New York: Atheneum Books for Young Readers, 2000. IL 5–8, RL 6.3

Hey, you see that crazy old man over there? The old guy in the dumpster? What do you suppose he's doing in there? Man, what a crackpot. But, you know what? That old guy over there is actually my grandfather. I can't tell the kids I'm with. They'd really have fun with that knowledge. So I just stare at Skelly and wish it didn't hurt so badly. Skelly wasn't always like this. He used to be fun and smart and the best guy in the world. He was everything to me. Then a few years ago the doctors told us that Skelly had a disease. It's a disease called Alzheimer's. I thought it meant that Skelly would forget where he put his keys or that he'd eaten. I had no way of knowing how bad the disease really is. Not only to the person who has it—to the whole family. See, my mother and I are the ones who are taking care of Skelly. We can't leave him alone any more. We can't trust him. I can't have any friends over any more either. Skelly might do something embarrassing in front of them, and I couldn't stand that. I still love Skelly, but it's just really hard now. Have any of your friends had a relative with Alzheimer's? Have you ever wondered what it's like to live with this disease? Well, I'll tell you.

Learning Extension Ideas

1. Alzheimer's disease is an illness that strikes elderly people. It is not a natural part of aging, and not all people come down with Alzheimer's. It is still not certain what causes it and what can be done to stop it. Have students research this disease and come up with a list of things that researchers think cause Alzheimer's.

2. Often, those who suffer from Alzheimer's think they are back at a long ago time in their lives. Many things may trigger this feeling. Often when we hear a certain song or smell a certain fragrance, we are reminded of the past. Have students test this. Pair them up, with one student in each pair blindfolded. The other should hold up an item so that the blindfolded student can smell it. Scents may include vanilla, cinnamon, flowers, onions, or grass. The blindfolded student should describe the smell and any memories it evokes. Have several substances on hand for the students to smell. What can we conclude from the results of this test?

Booktalk

Paulsen, Gary. *Hatchet.* New York: Simon & Schuster Books for Young Readers, 1987. IL 5–8, RL 6.3

This was not the way the summer was supposed to be. After my parents got a divorce, my dad got what they call "visitation" rights. That's what was supposed to happen this summer. But, instead, I am alone. And I'm trying to stay alive. My dad had arranged for me to fly up to see him. I was the only passenger on the small Cessna plane. Just me, Brian, and the pilot—Jim or Jake or something like that. When he suddenly had a heart attack, I was left alone to fly the plane and to land it. I didn't have the slightest idea of how to do either. By some miracle, I kept the plane flying and landed it in a lake. By some miracle, I lived through it. And now I'm alone—with nothing, trying to survive in the Canadian wilderness. No one knows where I am because we had gone off course when the pilot fell over. Is anyone looking for me? Will they think to look here? How will I survive until help arrives? And how many days will I have to wait? One day, two, a week, a month, or even longer? Can I survive? Could you?

Learning Extension Ideas

1. After the plane crash, Brian remembers that there is a survival kit on board the plane. He knows he must try to retrieve it. Have students list some of the things they think should been in an airplane survival kit. Remind them that they are traveling through the wilderness of Canada. List the items in order of importance. They can't take everything because space is limited, so they must narrow the list down to just 12 items. Compare the students' lists with those items in Brian's kit.

2. This experience has a profound effect on Brian. Have students explain how he is different after he is rescued, compared to before the accident.

Suggested Further Reading

Babbitt, Natalie. *Tuck Everlasting.* New York: Farrar, Straus & Giroux, 1975. IL 5–8, RL 5.9

The Tuck family is confronted with an agonizing situation when they discover that a 10-year-old girl and a malicious stranger now share their secret about a spring whose water prevents one from ever growing any older.

Bear, Greg. *Darwin's Radio.* New York: Ballantine, 1999. IL YA

Molecular biologist Kay Lang is a specialist in retroviruses. She teams up with virus hunter Christopher Dicken and anthropologist Mitch Rafelson in an attempt to trace the ancient source of a flu-like disease that is killing expectant mothers and their offspring and threatening the future of the human race.

Cook, Robin. *Outbreak.* New York: Berkley Books, 1988. IL YA, RL 9.0

When the director of a Los Angeles health maintenance clinic succumbs, along with seven patients, to an untreatable virus, Atlanta's Center for Disease Control goes on red alert. Dr. Melissa Blumenthal is sent to investigate.

Cushman, Karen. *Matilda Bone.* New York: Clarion, ©2000. IL 5–8, RL 6.1

Fourteen-year-old Matilda, an apprentice bonesetter and practitioner of medicine in a village in medieval England, tries to reconcile the various aspects of her life, both spiritual and practical.

Cushman, Karen. *The Midwife's Apprentice.* New York: Clarion Books, ©1995. IL YA, RL 6.0

In medieval England, a nameless, homeless girl is taken in by a sharp-tempered midwife. In spite of obstacles and hardship, the girl eventually gains the three things she most wants: a full belly, a contented heart, and a place in this world.

Haddix, Margaret Peterson. *Running Out of Time.* New York: Simon & Schuster Books for Young Readers, ©1995. IL 5–8, RL 6.4

When a diphtheria epidemic hits her 1840s-era village, 13-year-old Jessie discovers that it is actually a 1995 tourist site under unseen observation by heartless scientists. Now it's up to Jessie to escape the village and save the lives of the dying children.

Hesse, Karen. *A Time of Angels.* New York: Hyperion Books for Children, 2000. IL 5–8, RL 6.4

Sick with influenza during the 1918 epidemic and separated from her two sisters, a young Jewish girl living in Boston relies on the help of an old German man, and her visions of angels, to get better and to reunite with her family.

Mazer, Norma Fox. *After the Rain.* New York: William Morrow, 1987. IL YA, RL 5.3

After discovering that her grandfather is dying, 15-year-old Rachel gets to know him better than ever before, and she finds the experience bittersweet.

Nelson, O. T. *The Girl Who Owned a City.* Minneapolis, Minn.: Runestone Press, ©1995. IL 5–8, RL 5.1

When a plague sweeps over the earth, killing everyone except children under twelve, 10-year-old Lisa organizes a group to rebuild a new way of life.

Rubalcaba, Jill. *Saint Vitus' Dance.* New York: Clarion Books, ©1996. IL 5–8, RL 4.8

Fourteen-year-old Melanie must come to terms with her mother's incurable illness and the possibility that she herself may develop the same disease.

Physical Science

Booktalk

Hampton, Wilborn. *Meltdown: A Race Against Nuclear Disaster at Three Mile Island.* Cambridge, Mass.: Candlewick Press, 2001. IL 5–8, RL 8.9 (Nonfiction)

The trouble began around 4:00 in the morning. It was the end of a quiet shift at work. The workers had just completed a routine check of the dials and gauges, and everything checked out normal. Suddenly, alarms started to sound. Lights blinked off and on. The control panels lit up. The workers raced to try to figure out what was going on. The red lights on one of the control panels told them a horrifying tale: The water pumps had failed. Without water to cool the reactor, heat was rapidly building up in the brand new Unit No. 2 at Three Mile Island. What reads like a work of science fiction is actually the true story of what happened at Three Mile Island Nuclear Power Plant in 1979. Follow the events of that terrifying week when the world held its breath and waited for the unthinkable to happen: the total meltdown of a nuclear reactor.

Learning Extension Ideas

1. Have students research the nuclear accident at Chernobyl. They should be able to answer these questions: How was it different from the accident at Three Mile Island? What was the cause of the accident? What were the effects of the accident?

2. Have students research the uses of nuclear energy in medicine. Ask them: What are the benefits? What are the risks? Create a chart that lists the pros and cons of using nuclear energy in medicine.

Booktalk

O'Brien, Robert C. *Z for Zachariah.* New York: Aladdin, 1987. IL YA, RL 5.6

We've all heard the warnings. Nuclear war. Total annihilation. Could it ever really happen? I'll tell you, the answer is "yes." It happened months ago. For some reason, our little valley was spared. But from what we heard on the radio, the destruction was vast. Mom, Dad, and the neighbors went off to see if there were any survivors in Ogdensberg. My brother sneaked into the car so he could go, too. That was the last time I saw anyone else alive. Pretty soon, the radio stations went off the air. As far as I know, I'm the only person left alive in the entire world. One day, I see smoke in the distance. Of course, I've seen that before as the fires burned in the distance. But this is different. Each day, the small plume of smoke gets a little closer. I can't really explain how I feel. I'm excited but I am also afraid. Soon, I know that there is someone else alive in this world. He finds my house, but I hide, not knowing if it is safe to show myself. He is amazed that he has found a place not poisoned like the rest of the world. He is doing well until he decides to take a bath in the stream. I suppose I should have told him it was poisoned, but I still don't want to show myself. The stream makes him very sick, and I go down to the house to help him get well. He seems nice, at least at first. As the days go by, I begin to wonder if being alone is better than being with someone you don't know. I'm keeping this journal so that I can remember what happens. And maybe, if there are others, they can know too. Are you reading this? Have you survived?

Learning Extension Ideas

1. People talk about the threat of nuclear war. Ask students: How much of a possibility do you see of this happening in your lifetime? When the atom bomb was dropped in an effort to end World War II, many people were suddenly aware of the destructiveness of this technology. How do you think people's thinking about the threat of

nuclear war has changed in the past 50 years? Why do you think it has changed?

2. After World War II, the general public began to take precautions to save themselves in the event of a nuclear war. Some of these were naïve and extreme. Others were more realistic. Have students research the precautions that were endorsed by the government and create an informational brochure that could be given to the public during the 1950s with instructions on what to do in the event of an atom bomb dropping in their area. They should be sure to include only information that was available during the 1950s.

3. Have students pretend that they are a bomb shelter salesman. They should create a diagram and drawings of the bomb shelter they are trying to sell to a consumer. What points would they emphasize?

Booktalk

Taylor, Theodore. *The Bomb.* San Diego: Harcourt Brace, 1995. IL 5–8, RL 6.8

Sorry Rinamu, a teenager living on the Bikini Atoll, is about to turn 14, the traditional age for becoming a man on his island. But life has not been normal lately, so Sorry doesn't know what to expect. The Japanese occupied the island during the war. Now the Americans have arrived and "liberated" the people of Bikini Atoll. The Japanese are now gone. Can things get back to normal now that the war is over? Sorry doesn't think so. Even though the majority of the population thinks the Americans have come to help them, Sorry and his Uncle Abram see it differently. You see, the Americans want to use the atoll to experiment with atomic bombs. They have convinced the islanders to move to another island temporarily so that they can test a new weapon. The islanders have been assured that they can return to their home in two years. Sorry and his uncle are not convinced that the move will only be temporary. They devise a plan to stop the Americans from using their home to test atomic bombs. Will they succeed? What will happen to the displaced population?

Learning Extension Ideas

1. This book is based on a real event in U.S. history. At the time the author was in the military service, and he witnessed what happened on Bikini Atoll. Have students research this time and what really happened. Ask them: Were the islanders able to return to their homes? Why or why not?

2. Ask students: Why did the United States choose the island as a test site? How many bombs were dropped on Bikini Atoll? How did the atomic testing affect the environment of the island? What lasting effects are seen today? Has the United States been able to clean up the atoll after the testing? Have students research the area to find the answers to these questions.

Booktalk

Zindel, Paul. *The Gadget.* New York: HarperCollins, ©2001. IL 5–8, RL 5.8

London during the Second World War was not a safe place to live. Stephen is sent away from his home in England to join his father in the United States. He travels to New Mexico, wondering if he and his father will be able to get along. What he finds is that his father is working on a secret project and has little time for Stephen. The scientists are all referred to by code names, and no one will talk about the project. No one except Dr. Soifer. He tells Stephen of the devastation that will be brought about by the "Gadget." Will Stephen discover the secret "Gadget?" And just why did Stephen's father forbid him to be friends with the Russian boy on base?

Learning Extension Ideas

1. There were many scientists involved in the Manhattan Project. Have students choose one and write a short biography of the person. They should indicate how that person was involved in the development of the atomic bomb.

2. The dropping of the atomic bomb effectively ended the war. Ask students: What do you think the reaction of the American people was when they heard of the devastation in Japan? Write a newspaper article telling the public about the bomb and the destruction it caused.

Suggested Further Reading

Barron, T. A. *Heartlight.* New York: TOR, 1994. IL 5–8, RL 6.2

Kate and her grandfather use one of his inventions, combining psychic power with quantum physics, to travel faster than the speed of light on a mission to save the sun from a premature death.

Coerr, Eleanor. *Mieko and the Fifth Treasure.* New York: G. P. Putnam's Sons, ©1993. IL 3–6, RL 6.2

Staying with her grandparents after the atomic bomb has been dropped on Nagasaki, 10-year-old Mieko feels that the happiness in her heart has departed forever and she will no longer be able to produce a beautiful drawing for the contest at school.

Duffey, Betsy. *Coaster.* New York: Puffin Books, 1996. IL 5–8, RL 5.5

While secretly building a roller coaster in the woods, 12-year-old Hart tries to come to terms with his parents' divorce and his mother's new relationship with a television weatherman.

Gallant, Roy A. *The Ever-Changing Atom.* New York: Benchmark Books, 1999, ©2000. IL 5–8, RL 8.0

Introduces atoms, the tiny particles that make up everything in the world, discussing their different parts, how they were discovered, and how they can be used as a source of energy.

Golding, William. *Lord of the Flies: A Novel.* New York: Perigee, ©1954. IL YA, RL 5.0

Stranded on an island while an atomic war destroys the rest of the world, a group of young boys revert to savagery as they struggle to survive.

Hall, Lynn. *If Winter Comes.* New York: Atheneum Books for Young Readers, ©1986. IL YA, RL 8.2

As an escalating world crisis makes the threat of nuclear war imminent, teenager Meredith and her boyfriend Barry draw closer to each other and to other people important to them during what could be the last weekend of their lives.

Hesse, Karen. *Phoenix Rising.* New York: Henry Holt, 1994. IL 5–8, RL 4.8

Thirteen-year-old Nyle learns about relationships and death when 15-year-old Ezra, who was exposed to radiation leaked from a nearby nuclear plant, comes to stay at her grandmother's Vermont farmhouse.

Sherrow, Victoria. *The Making of the Atom Bomb.* San Diego: Lucent Books, ©2000. IL 5–8, RL 6.8

Discusses various topics connected with the production of the atom bomb. Includes the development of nuclear energy, work on atomic weapons at Los Alamos and other sites, and the decision to use the first atomic bomb during World War II.

Wiese, Jim. *Roller Coaster Science: 50 Wet, Wacky, Wild, Dizzy Experiments About Things Kids Like Best.* New York: John Wiley, ©1994. IL 5–8, RL 6.5

Describes the science behind such amusements as roller coasters, swings, bumper cars, hot dogs, curve balls, and more. Includes easy experiments.

Yep, Laurence. *Hiroshima: A Novella.* New York: Scholastic, ©1995. IL 3–6, RL 4.0

Describes the dropping of the atomic bomb on Hiroshima, Japan, particularly as it affects Sachi, who becomes one of the Hiroshima Maidens.

Nature of Science Inquiry

Booktalk

Crichton, Michael. *Jurassic Park: A Novel.* New York: Alfred A. Knopf, 1990. IL YA, RL 7.3

Just because you can do something doesn't mean that you should do it. The scientists who find some dinosaur DNA know this but can't help getting excited about the possibility of cloning a real dinosaur. What begins as a compelling idea takes off. The cloning of one dinosaur blossoms into the population of a whole island of dinosaurs. It's all been financed by billionaire John Hammond. The island is to become an amusement park where visitors can see real dinosaurs up close and personal. Can you imagine anything so extraordinary? What a great experience! Or is it? It seems the dinosaurs have other ideas!

Learning Extension Ideas

1. Ask students: Is Jurassic Park possible? Why or why not?

2. Ask students: How do archaeologist learn about animals that are extinct? What do they look for in an animal skeleton or fossil? What clues do they get?

Booktalk

Haddix, Margaret Peterson. *Turnabout.* New York: Simon & Schuster Books for Young Readers, 2000. IL YA, RL 7.0

Do you ever think about getting old? Not just into your twenties or thirties, but really old. Maybe around 100 years old. If you live that long, you may find that your body doesn't work like it used to. You won't see as well, you won't hear as well. You may not even be able to get around. Now, what if you are 100 years old and someone offers you a chance to be young again? Do you think you would take the person up on it? Well, that's the choice that the characters in this book have made. They have decided to be part of an experiment to turn back aging. Instead of getting a year older each year, they get a year younger. Instead of turning 101, they turn 99. Sounds pretty good, eh? Well, things are not always what they seem. As the characters become younger, they find they must pay a price for their youth, a price that even the doctors hadn't anticipated. To some, it simply isn't worth it. Find out what happens to the chosen few who are given a chance to be young again in Turnabout. Would you be willing to pay the price?

Learning Extension Ideas

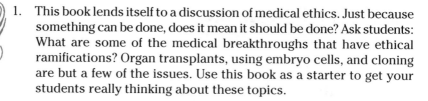

1. This book lends itself to a discussion of medical ethics. Just because something can be done, does it mean it should be done? Ask students: What are some of the medical breakthroughs that have ethical ramifications? Organ transplants, using embryo cells, and cloning are but a few of the issues. Use this book as a starter to get your students really thinking about these topics.

2. Have students discuss why people would want to stay young. Have students evaluate the images they find in newspapers, magazines, and other popular media. What age are the people in the ads? What age is the intended audience? What product is being sold? Is there a correlation between the ad's models and the ad's intended audience? What conclusions can be drawn?

Booktalk

Kaye, Marilyn. *Pursuing Amy.* New York: Bantam Books, 1998. IL 5–8, RL 7.5

Amy Chandler looks like any other 12-year-old girl. On the surface, she seems like an average middle school girl. But it is soon obvious that she is different. She can solve advanced math problems without any difficulty. She is a natural athlete who excels at multiple sports. She is not an average middle school girl. As a matter of fact, she has a very unusual background. She was created in a lab. She is a product of cloning. She tries desperately to keep her secret from getting out because she wants to live like an average girl in her town. But as her talents begin to advance, she wonders if she will be able to keep her secret. Is there anyone she can trust? Who are those people who are after her? And what do they want?

Learning Extension Ideas

1. Cloning is still a fairly new technology. Although it has been discussed for a long time, it has only been performed successfully during the past decade. Have the students research the uses of cloning. How do scientists envision using cloning to help society?

2. There is much debate about the ethics of cloning. The use of cloning on plants seems to be much less controversial than cloning animals. Have students take a position on the controversy and write an editorial stating their opinions.

Booktalk

Verne, Jules. *Twenty Thousand Leagues Under the Sea.* New York: Bantam Books, 1981. IL YA, RL 7.0

There are reports of a strange sea monster living in the ocean. A scientist and his party set off to find the creature, but their ship is destroyed in a massive explosion. Amazingly, they are rescued by that very same sea monster! It turns out to be a submarine. The year is 1866, and submarines are virtually unheard of, especially a submarine as advanced as the *Nautilus*. The shipwrecked crew is imprisoned on the *Nautilus* for eight months. During that time, they take part in a series of amazing adventures. Although intrigued by the science of the *Nautilus* and the inventions of its captain, Nemo, the three survivors try to escape. Join these characters on their adventures *Twenty Thousand Leagues Under the Sea.*

Learning Extension Ideas

1. This book was written in 1870. Jules Verne was able to imagine many modern inventions that were not in existence then. Ask students: What are some of the machines that were not available at that time? Which ones have since come into existence?

2. Have students imagine themselves as one of the sailors taken aboard the submarine. They should write a letter back home trying to explain the unusual events they are experiencing. They should be sure to describe the sea monsters and draw a picture of one to show their friends back home.

Booktalk

Wells, H. G. *The Time Machine.* New York: Bantam Books, 1991. IL YA, RL 7.4

Join us, if you will, for a quiet dinner party. Several friends have gathered and are having a good time. The conversation covers many topics. But then, the host begins to tell the others about his theory of time travel. He goes into great detail, but his friends don't believe him. He shows them a small model of a time machine he has built and demonstrates the device using a cigar as the time traveler. He pushes the lever forward and the machine disappears. His friends believe it's a trick and laugh it off. Everyone scoffs at his rantings. After everyone leaves, the scientist goes into another room where he has built a full-sized time machine. He climbs in, pushes the lever forward, and begins a journey into time that no one could have foreseen. Now the adventures begin.

Learning Extension Ideas

1. In this novel, H. G. Wells offers us his version of what the world will be like in the future. Have students rewrite the description of the future. What do they think the world will be like? Will there be distinct classes of humans as there are in this novel?

2. Have students pretend they have their own time machine that they can control. They should choose a destination, both a time and a place. Have them write a narrative about why they have chosen that destination and also tell about what they see, hear, and experience while there.

Suggested Further Reading

Cook, Robin. *Outbreak.* New York: Berkley Books, 1988, ©1987. IL YA, RL 9.0

When the director of a Los Angeles health maintenance clinic succumbs, along with seven patients, to an untreatable virus, Atlanta's Center for Disease Control goes on red alert. Dr. Melissa Blumenthal is sent to investigate.

Dickinson, Peter. *Eva.* New York: Dell, 1990. IL YA, RL 7.0

After a terrible accident, a young girl wakes up to discover that she has been given the body of a chimpanzee.

DuPrau, Jeanne. *Cloning.* San Diego: Lucent Books, 1999, ©2000. IL 5–8, RL 8.0

Discusses the methods, regulation, and ethics of cloning in relation to agriculture, medicine, endangered species, and human beings.

George, Jean Craighead. *The Fire Bug Connection: An Ecological Mystery.* New York: HarperTrophy, 1995. IL 5–8, RL 4.7

Twelve-year-old Maggie receives European firebugs for her birthday, but when they fail to metamorphose and explode instead, she uses scientific reasoning to determine the cause of their strange deaths.

Haddix, Margaret Peterson. *Running Out of Time.* New York: Simon & Schuster Books for Young Readers, 1995. IL 5–8, RL 6.4

When a diphtheria epidemic hits her 1840s-era village, 13-year-old Jessie discovers that it is actually a 1995 tourist site under unseen observation by heartless scientists, and it's up to Jessie to escape the village and save the lives of the dying children.

Kerner, Charlotte. *Blueprint.* Minneapolis, Minn.: Lerner, 2000. IL YA

Siri Sellin, one of the first human clones, writes a bitter memoir of her childhood as the daughter of a famous and self-absorbed composer.

Lasky, Kathryn. *Star Split.* New York: Hyperion Paperbacks for Children, 2001, ©1999. IL 5–8, RL 6.0

In 3038, 13-year-old Darci uncovers an underground movement to save the human race from genetic enhancement technology.

Levy, Debbie. *Medical Ethics.* San Diego: Lucent Books, ©2001. IL 5–8, RL 7.7

Discusses the ethics of experimental treatments, genetic engineering, the availability of medical information about individuals, organ transplants, and assisted suicide.

Peel, John. *Revolution.* New York: Scholastic, ©2000. IL 5–8, RL 6.4

In the year 2099, the status quo is threatened by a revolution that originates in the Underworld and the prison on Ice.

Wells, Donna Koren. *Biotechnology.* New York: Benchmark
Books, ©1996. IL 5–8, RL 6.5

Describes the history and applications of biotechnology, focusing on how
scientists develop new organisms by altering the genetic makeup of living
things.

8 ♪ The Arts

Introduction

In school the study of the arts includes dance, music, theater arts, and visual arts, but the arts are also part of our daily life. They are so deeply embedded in our everyday experiences that we may not even be aware of their presence.

Today the study of the arts often involves integration with other subject areas, such as math and social studies. Music, dance, drama, and visual arts are often taught in conjunction with other disciplines and are taught differently, sometimes nonverbally rather than verbally or emotionally rather than logically.

Through the arts we learn new ways to appreciate our world, to better express ourselves, and to communicate with others. They play a significant role in creating cultures and building civilizations. They can offer avenues to conflict resolution, teamwork, and sensitivity to others.

In our daily lives, the arts also offer personal fulfillment and are part of our leisure activities. Time spent at movies, concerts, plays, or dances is time we enjoy. Because of this, many young people feel a special connection to the arts, so books with art themes are sure to be a hit with some hard to reach learners.

The value of the arts in our society is undeniable. They connect new generations to those that have gone before. Knowing about, understanding, and appreciating a variety of world cultures and historic periods are just some of the benefits of arts education.

In this section, we explore books dealing with various arts themes. The chapter is divided into music, visual arts, and performing arts, which includes both dance and theater.

RL = Reading Level   *IL = Interest Level*

Music

Booktalk

Doucet, Sharon Arms. *Fiddle Fever.* New York: Clarion Books, 2000. IL 3–6, RL 4.8

The year is 1914. Felix LeBlanc lives with his family—and what a family it is. Grandpa died and left his estate to Felix's family and Uncle Nonc, but Uncle Nonc hasn't been around for four years. That makes the family very angry. You see, Grandpa left Uncle Nonc the big house and the high land since he is the oldest son. Felix's family got the small house on the hardpan clay along the Louisiana bayou. But Nonc got "fiddle fever" and went off to New Orleans, leaving the big house empty and the land untended. Nonc's sister Maman, Papa, and the rest of the family have struggled to make a living. But now Nonc is back, and things will be different. His fiddle playing creates a longing in Felix. Felix wonders if maybe he's caught "fiddle fever." Felix's mother forbids him to learn to play the fiddle because she is afraid he will turn out to be a useless fiddle player like Uncle Nonc. But, can you be cured once you catch "fiddle fever?"

Learning Extension Ideas

1. Ask students: Have you ever felt you were born to do something? No matter how many people tell you that you can't or shouldn't do it, you just know you will risk anything to do it? Write a narrative about it. What have you done about it?

2. Felix is forbidden to have a violin. He decides that only way to get one is to make it himself. Ask students: What do you think of his home-made fiddle? Have students research how instruments are made and write about the steps Felix would have to take to make his own.

Booktalk

Krull, Kathleen. *Lives of the Musicians: Good Times, Bad Times (and What the Neighbors Thought).* San Diego: Harcourt Brace, ©1993. IL 5–8, RL 6.3 (Nonfiction)

Do any of you like to listen to music? Do you know anything about the people behind the music? The composers and the musicians? There are some really outrageous stories about their wild parties and eccentric life styles. Can you guess who some of these musicians might be? One musician's music provoked riots, and the police were called in to control the crowds. Another musician's music was condemned as immoral and addictive. What about the musician who left blood on the piano keys? The answers may surprise you. It was Stravinsky whose music led to riots. Scott Joplin's music was labeled immoral and addictive. And it was George Gershwin who often left blood on the piano keys. Learn about these famous musicians and more about the men and women behind the classics in *Lives of the Musicians*.

Learning Extension Ideas

1. Ask students: How did reading this book change your opinion of classical music? Create a script for one of the musicians for a *Behind the Music* program on the VH1 channel.

2. Have students choose one of the musicians in the book and create a mobile for that musician. Each item on the mobile should represent a fact about the musician. They should be sure to use some of the information found in the book.

Booktalk

Levine, Gail Carson. *Dave at Night.* New York: HarperCollins, 1999. IL 3–6, RL 4.0

Life is not going too well for Dave. As a matter of fact, this may be the worst day in his life. First, his father died from falling off the roof of a house. Then his stepmother told him she was giving him up 'cause she can't feed him anymore. To top it all off, no one in his family will take him in. What's a poor kid to do? Well, for Dave there is just one choice. He's hustled off to the HHB, the Hebrew Home for Boys. It's certainly not the best place to live—far from it. Things may be bad for Dave, but some good things are bound to happen, and they do. For one thing, he meets an unusual collection of people from the city, including a vocalist from Harlem. Harlem in the 1920s was the best place to be for music. Join Dave and his collection of friends in *Dave at Night*.

Learning Extension Ideas

1. The music, art, and poetry of the Harlem Renaissance are well known. Ask students: If Dave kept a scrapbook of all the people he met and the activities around him, what would be in it? Have them create a scrapbook that might have been kept by Dave, using magazines, newspapers, and the Internet to collect information.

2. Borrow some music from the 1920s for the students to listen to. Have them write a narrative about how the music makes them feel. Ask students: What do they like about the music? What don't they like about it? How is it different from popular music today?

Booktalk

Wolff, Virginia. *The Mozart Season.* New York: Scholastic, 1993. IL YA, RL 5.0

Take a trip inside the mind of a 12-year-old violin student spending the summer preparing for a competition of the fourth violin concerto by Mozart. The youngest contestant, Allegra, spends a lot of time practicing, but she also wonders how she has gotten her where she is. Along the way, there was an eccentric opera star with a tragic past and a bag person who has lost waltz trees and loves to dance. If you love music, you'll love this story.

Learning Extension Ideas

1. While Allegra is studying and practicing for the audition, she learns many important lessons. Have students write a narrative about what Allegra learns about how she can make the concerto her own. Have them use a familiar tune and write their own lyrics to go along with it.

2. Allegra sacrifices many things to achieve her goal. She works very hard and devotes herself to doing well at the audition. Ask students: Have you ever cared about something so much that you worked extra hard for it? Write a poem about your passion. Then turn your poem into a rap to present to the class.

3. Allegra's music teacher was a great inspiration for her. Ask students: Have you ever had an adult that was special to you? Perhaps a teacher, a coach, a scout leader? Have students create a thank-you card for that person. Have them also come up with a song that they feel reflects the qualities of that person.

Booktalk

Yolen, Jane. *Boots and the Seven Leaguers: A Rock-and-Troll Novel.* San Diego: Harcourt, 2000. IL 5–8, RL 5.6

Do you have a favorite pop band? Have you ever gone to one of their concerts? Would you like to? Well, this is a story about the band Boots and the Seven Leaguers, the greatest band in the world. They are not just the greatest band in the world; they are the greatest crossover band in the Kingdom. Boots plays in the Out, but their roots are in the Kingdom. Since they made it big in the Out, they only play the Kingdom once a year. If they don't return once a year, they will find that they can never come back. Some say that staying away for the entire run of the sun locks you out of the Kingdom, and you will have to live with the humans forever. Humans are an interesting bunch, but no one wants to live with them forever. Now Gog, a young troll, and his best friend, Pook, have decided to disguise themselves as roadies for the band to get into the concert. Will they get to see Boots and the band perform the hit from their latest CD? Join Gog and Pook on the adventure of their lives in *Boots and the Seven Leaguers.*

Learning Extension Ideas

1. Gog and Pook try to get into the concert by signing on as roadies. Ask students: What are roadies, and what do they do? Do you think this sounds like a good job?

2. Have students work in groups and pretend that they are entertainment television reporters assigned to interview Boots and the Seven Leaguers. Assign the roles of the band, the reporter, and others that may be interesting to interview (e.g., fans, roadies, family). Students should turn in a script as well as acting out the interview. The interview can be performed live or recorded.

3. Have students think of some of the popular bands today. If they were really from the Kingdom, what type of character would they be: troll, Pan, fairy, etc.?

Suggested Further Reading

Dahlberg, Maurine F. *Play to the Angel.* New York: Farrar, Straus & Giroux, 2000. IL 5–8, RL 6.3

In Vienna in 1938, in the shadow of an increasingly dangerous Nazi Germany, 12-year-old Greta pursues her dream of becoming a concert pianist like her dead brother Kurt, despite a lack of support from her widowed mother.

Henry, Chad. *Dogbreath Victorious.* New York: Holiday House, ©1999. IL YA, RL 4.8

Dogbreath, Tim's alternative Seattle grunge rock band, enters a major battle of the bands contest. They are beaten by The Angry Housewives, a new group fronted by Tim's mother.

Hrdlitschka, Shelley. *Beans on Toast.* Victoria, B.C.: Orca, ©1998. IL 5–8, RL 6.9

Madison, unhappy since her parents' divorce, is having a difficult time making friends at band camp. The exciting events of that two-week period conspire to draw her out of her self-imposed solitude.

O'Connor, Barbara. *Beethoven in Paradise.* New York: Farrar, Straus & Giroux, 1997. IL 5–8, RL 4.2

Martin longs to be a musician, and with the encouragement of two very different friends, he eventually is able to defy his mean-hearted father and accept himself and the talent within him.

Paterson, Katherine. *Come Sing, Jimmy Jo.* New York: E. P. Dutton, ©1985. IL 5–8, RL 4.9

When his family becomes a successful country music group and makes him a featured singer, 11-year-old James has to deal with big changes in all aspects of his life—even his name.

Pinkwater, Daniel Manus. *Lizard Music.* New York: Bantam Doubleday Dell Books for Young Readers, 1996, ©1976. IL 5–8, RL 6.9

When left to take care of himself, a young boy becomes involved with a community of intelligent lizards who tell him about a little-known invasion from outer space.

Powell, Randy. *Tribute to Another Dead Rock Star.* New York: Farrar, Straus & Giroux, 1999. IL YA, RL 4.4

For a tribute to his mother, a dead rock star, 15-year-old Grady returns to Seattle, where he faces his mixed feelings for his retarded younger half-brother Louie while pondering his own future.

Thesman, Jean. *Cattail Moon.* Boston: Houghton Mifflin, ©1994. IL 5–8, RL 5.3

Unable to deal with her mother's disregard of her interest in a musical career, 15-year-old Julia leaves Seattle to live with her father and grandmother near the Cascade Mountains. There she encounters a ghost who helps her make important decisions about her future.

Willey, Margaret. *Facing the Music.* New York: Bantam Doubleday Dell Books for Young Readers, ©1996. IL YA, RL 4.6

Through her love of music and membership in her brother's band, 16-year-old Lisa learns to deal with her feelings of abandonment following her mother's death.

Wilson, Nancy Hope. *Becoming Felix.* New York: Farrar, Straus & Giroux, ©1996. IL 5–8, RL 5.2

Worried about the difficulties on his family's Massachusetts dairy farm, 12-year-old JJ is willing to give up on his dreams of becoming a great clarinet player and on his friendship with a new Jewish classmate who shares his love of music.

Visual Arts

Booktalk

Bunting, Eve. *The Memory String.* New York: Clarion Books, 2000. IL K–3, RL 2.5

Laura sits in the back yard and pulls out a string of buttons. Each one contains a memory. There is one from her great-grandmother's first grown-up dress. There are buttons from great-aunts and from cousins. There is one from her father's uniform when he came back from the Gulf War. There is a button from the nightgown her mother was wearing when she died. Laura loudly recites the meanings as she fingers each button. She is deliberately trying to hurt her new stepmother by talking about the memories. Oh, how she misses her mother. Oh, how she wishes her father had never remarried. When the string breaks and the buttons are scattered throughout the yard, Laura learns an important lesson. Memories are important, but making new ones is just as important. Share Laura's memories and her discoveries in *The Memory String*.

Learning Extension Ideas

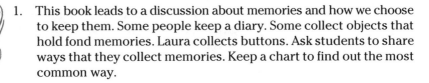

1. This book leads to a discussion about memories and how we choose to keep them. Some people keep a diary. Some collect objects that hold fond memories. Laura collects buttons. Ask students to share ways that they collect memories. Keep a chart to find out the most common way.

2. Have the students create paper beads to celebrate classroom memories. The beads can be added to a classroom string throughout the year as memorable events happen. Students can use newspaper, wrapping paper, wallpaper samples, magazine pages, or anything colorful. Have them cut a triangle piece that is 1 inch wide and 11 inches long. Beginning with the wider end, they should roll the paper triangle around a pencil. They can paint the bead with clear glue and let it dry before stringing the beads.

Booktalk

Fleischmann, Paul. *Whirligig.* New York: Henry Holt, 1998. IL YA, RL 4.9

Brent Bishop is new in town. This isn't the first time his family has moved to a new place, but it still seems so hard fit in. When Brent is invited to a party at the home of one of the most popular kids in town, he thinks he's finally made it. Then he finds out that he isn't actually invited. A kid he knows has been invited and Brent is just giving him a ride. The party turns out to be a disaster. No one told Brent about the dress code. Then the girl Brent likes embarrasses him by rejecting him and telling everyone what a loser he is. Brent leaves the party and drives home. He's a little drunk, a lot depressed. Suddenly he decides he doesn't want to live anymore, so he shuts his eyes and waits for the crash. Brent lives, but he has killed a young girl. Her parents decide that instead of going to jail, Brent's punishment will be a bit more unconventional. Brent doesn't really understand what they are aiming at, but goes along with the deal. What can this accomplish? Who can possibly benefit from Brent's efforts?

Learning Extension Ideas

1. While in Maine, Brent Bishop describes himself as sort of an artist. He was a whirligig artist. Ask students: How did the whirligigs affect people who came across them? How did they affect Brent? What did Brent learn about himself and about the world itself?

2. Brent describes the world as a giant whirligig. Ask students: What does he mean by that?

3. Ask students: How does art affect our lives? What would life be like without art?

4. Have students create whirligigs out of construction paper. Students will need to design a two-sided object. "Arms" can be attached using brackets. Alternatively, have students draw a design for a whirligig.

Booktalk

Ingold, Jeanette. *Pictures, 1918.* San Diego: Harcourt Brace, 1998. IL 5–8, RL 7.3

Asia watches in horror as the chicken coop goes up in flames. Her pet rabbit is in there. She has managed to save the kittens and turtle, but the rabbit can't be saved. As she mourns for her beloved pet, she wishes she had a good picture of him so she could remember that image and not the last few moments of his life. When she saw the Autographic camera for sale at the drug store, she knew she had to have it even though it was very expensive. Could she earn enough money to buy it? If she did, could she ever learn how to use it?

Learning Extension Ideas

1. In the year 1918, the world was at war. There was also a major flu epidemic that was killing thousands of people. Ask students: How does this historical background affect Asia's desire to learn to use the camera?

2. Asia finds she learns more about life through the camera lens than she does any other way. Ask students: How is that possible? What can she learn?

3. There's an old saying that every picture tells a story. Have a variety of photographs available. These can be actual photographs or printouts from Web sites. The American Memory Project Web site (http://memory.loc.gov) has a wonderful collection to choose from. Give each student one photograph (or have each choose one from a collection). Have students analyze what they are seeing and write a short story about what is being portrayed.

Booktalk

Lisle, Janet Taylor. *The Art of Keeping Cool.* New York: Atheneum Books for Young Readers, 2000. IL 5–8, RL 6.2

Robert is so proud of his father, one of the first pilots to be sent to England to help fight in the war. It's February 1942, and the United States is just entering the war that has been raging in Europe for the past few years. It wasn't until December that the United States was officially involved. Now Robert and his mother are left in Ohio and are trying to maintain the family farm. With so many men going off to join the army, there is no way to hire enough men to help with the farm. Robert's mother makes a decision that will forever change their lives. She has decided to take Robert and his sister back East to live near Robert's father's parents. When they arrive in Rhode Island, Robert meets a cousin he never knew existed. Elliott is the same age as Robert, but the two boys are quite different. Actually, Elliott is different from most boys his age. He is timid, even fearful, and very quiet. But when Robert gets to know him, he finds that Elliott is a gifted artist. Elliott doesn't want anyone to know about his talent, though. He just isn't confident enough in his talent and doesn't want anyone to make fun of his art. Robert is amazed at how good Elliott is. As the months go by, Robert begins to realize that things are not always as they seem. Sometimes, we must look beyond ourselves to see how things are. Robert learns a great deal from Elliott and from a German painter who has taken refuge in the woods. Often what can't be said in words can be shown clearly in art.

Learning Extension Ideas

1. Elliott tells Robert that he draws because if you do it right, the real thing gets caught and can't hurt you. Ask students: What does he mean by this?

2. Abel Hoffman tells Elliott and Robert about the Nazi persecution of artists. Ask students: Why would the Nazis be afraid of art? How can art, music, and literature influence society?

3. Abel Hoffman is described as an Impressionist painter. Have students view photographs of some Impressionist paintings and describe what they see, what they think the artist is saying, and how it makes them feel.

Booktalk

Stanley, Diane. *Michelangelo.* New York: HarperCollins, 2000. IL 3–6, RL 5.8 (Nonfiction)

You have all probably heard of the famous artist, Michelangelo. And you may know that he lived during a time in history known as the Renaissance. During that time, Europe was a haven for artists of all kinds. The city of Florence, Italy, was home to many artists, but Michelangelo was by far the most famous. This book describes Michelangelo's life, which wasn't a very happy one. It also shows many of his most famous sculptures. Michelangelo didn't limit his work to sculpting. He also painted and was an architect. There is a story that during that time, a young man created a statue in the Greek style, buried it in the ground to give it an antique look and then sold it to a wealthy art collector as a genuine Greek statue. When the art collector discovered the forgery, he went to Florence looking for the young man who had created the statue. He was not angry; he just wanted to meet the artist who had such skill that he could fool the art dealers. The young man was Michelangelo. When Michelangelo was near death, he stated that his work was of little value and that it might last for a little while. How could he have known that even now, 500 years later, we still view him as one of the most accomplished artists of all time?

Learning Extension Ideas

1. Have students create their own sculptures with clay or by using a bar of bath soap and a small knife. They can create animals, people, places, and so forth.

2. One of Michelangelo's most famous works is the ceiling of the Sistine Chapel. Michelangelo worked hour after hour lying on his back on a scaffold. Have students create their own ceiling artwork, then display it on the ceiling of the classroom or hallway.

Suggested Further Reading

Bowler, Tim. *River Boy.* New York: Margaret K. McElderry, 2000, ©1997. IL 5–8, RL 5.2

Knowing that he is dying, Jess's grandfather insists on returning to the river he had known as a boy to finish a special painting and fulfill a lifelong dream.

Coatsworth, Elizabeth Jane. *The Cat Who Went to Heaven.* New York: Aladdin, 1990. IL 5–8, RL 6.6

A little cat comes to the home of a poor Japanese artist and, by humility and devotion, brings him good fortune.

Deaver, Julie Reece. *Chicago Blues.* New York: HarperCollins, ©1995. IL 5–8, RL 5.4

Lissa, a 17-year-old art student living on her own in Chicago, must raise her 11-year-old sister when their alcoholic mother becomes incapable of caring for her.

Holmes, Barbara Ware. *Following Fake Man.* New York: Alfred A. Knopf; distributed by Random House, ©2001. IL 5–8, RL 6.9

During his summer in Maine, 12-year-old Homer, together with his new friend Roger, is determined to find the truth about himself, his long-dead father, and a mysterious costumed man.

Mack, Tracy. *Drawing Lessons.* New York: Scholastic, 2000. IL 5–8, RL 7.5

Twelve-year-old Rory begins to lose the passion for making art that she shares with her father after she finds him kissing his female model and fears for the safety of her parents' marriage.

Mackall, Dandi Daley. *Portrait of Lies.* Nashville, Tenn.: Tommy Nelson, ©2000. IL 5–8, RL 5.2

Encouraged by her close friends and a mystery supporter in cyberspace, Jamie decides to enter a contest to win an art camp scholarship despite her own lack of confidence in her artistic ability.

Mazzio, Joann. *Leaving Eldorado.* Boston: Houghton Mifflin, ©1993. IL YA, RL 4.8

In the late 1890s, 14-year-old Maude is abandoned by her gold-mad father in the small New Mexico Territory mining town of Eldorado. Now she struggles to survive and to hold onto her dream of becoming an artist.

Molina Llorente, Pilar. *The Apprentice.* New York: Farrar, Straus & Giroux, 1994. IL 5–8, RL 6.3

Working as an artist's apprentice in Renaissance Florence, 13-year-old Arduino makes a discovery that may cost him the chance to become a painter.

Nolan, Han. *Send Me Down a Miracle.* San Diego: Harcourt Brace, ©1996. IL YA, RL 5.3

A sleepy, God-fearing Southern town erupts in chaos when a flamboyant artist from New York City returns to her birthplace for an artistic experiment.

Paulsen, Gary. *The Monument.* New York: Dell, 1993, ©1991. IL YA, RL 4.9

Thirteen-year-old Rocky is self-conscious about the braces on her leg. Her life changes when a remarkable artist comes to her small Kansas town to design a war memorial.

Performing Arts

Booktalk

Blackwood, Gary. *The Shakespeare Stealer.* New York: Dutton Children's Books, 1998. IL 5–8, RL 5.5

Young Widge is an orphan growing up in sixteenth-century England. He spends his first seven years in an orphanage and sometimes allows himself to dream about having a family. At age seven, he is apprenticed to Dr. Bright, who is anything but a kind man. Dr. Bright has developed a form of short-hand writing and is determined that Widge master it. This shorthand allows

Widge to write down what people are saying as they are saying it. Because Widge is a bright young man, he masters the shorthand in about a year. But when Widge finds out what Dr. Bright wants him to do with this shorthand, Widge knows it's wrong. Still, how can he refuse his master? Then Widge is sold to a new master. It turns out that the new master is in charge of a troop of actors and they are in need of new plays to perform. The new master sends Widge to London to steal a play by William Shakespeare. Again, Widge knows that this is wrong, but how can he say no, especially to a man who threatens to kill him if he doesn't get the play?

Learning Extension Ideas

1. During Shakespeare's time, it was not uncommon for acting troupes to steal plays from each other. To try to prevent this, the owner of the troupe would have only one copy of the script, which was kept under lock and key. Actors were told their lines in short parts. They were never given copies of the play. There were no laws to protect the playwrights. Ask students: What protects authors today from people copying their words? How does it work? Students may need to do some research to find this out.

2. Dr. Bright has devised a new written language code for a person to write quicker. Have students devise their own written language. They should provide an example of the language, a translation, a message to be decoded by a classmate (complete with answer key), and the purpose of the new language. The purpose does not have to be to speed up writing; students should be creative about the purpose.

Booktalk

Calhoun, Dia. *Aria of the Sea.* Delray Beach, Fla.: Winslow Press, 2000. IL YA, RL 5.0

Cerinthe Gale of Normost has a dream. She dreams of becoming a dancer in the Royal School. This was the wish of her mother from her deathbed. Now the time has come for Cerinthe to audition for the school. Being a commoner, she is not sure she even has a chance to be chosen for the Queen's school, but during the audition, she feels she is one of the best dancers trying out. When she is not asked back for the third round of tryouts, she cannot believe it. She just knows she did better than the 15 girls chosen for the third round of auditions. Determined to learn to dance, Cerinthe gets a job in the laundry at the school. She hopes she can at least be around the great teachers and hopes to be able to afford to take lessons some day. Is this the end of Cerinthe's dream of becoming a great dancer?

Learning Extension Ideas

1. Cerinthe suffers from homesickness. Of course, that is only part of her sadness. Ask students: Have you ever gone away from home and suffered from homesickness? What was it like? Describe in writing the feeling and what you did about it.

2. Have students create a poster that announces the Princess's ballet. They should be sure to list cast and any special information about the performance. The poster should be illustrated.

Booktalk

Glover, Savion. *Savion: My Life in Tap.* New York: William Morrow, 2000. IL YA, RL 5.9 (Nonfiction)

Savion Glover made tap dance cool again. Savion began to play drums at a very early age. He eventually decided that his feet were the drums and his tap shoes were the sticks. He began concentrating on tap instead of drums. After being discovered, Savion had a successful career on the stage as well as television. He was even a regular cast member of *Sesame Street*! Savion has taken an established art form and remade it as his own. His feet are his voice as he performs hip-hop music. This book tells of his life, his career, and his hopes for the future. Find out more about this remarkable young man in *Savion: My Life in Tap.*

Learning Extension Ideas

1. Ask students: How is tap dancing different from modern dance or ballet?

2. Savion was instrumental in developing the show *Bring in da noise, Bring in da funk*. The book tells us the background of the musical. Have students compare this musical to the Irish musical *Riverdance*. Ask them: What was the underlying concept to both? How are they similar? How are they different? More information about *Riverdance* is available at http://www.riverdance.com.

3. Savion believes he was born to dance. Ask students: What do you think you were born to do?

Booktalk

Vail, Rachel. *Please, Please, Please.* New York: Scholastic, 1998. IL 5–8, RL 7.8

CJ is just your typical seventh grader. She's been best friends with Morgan forever. Lately, though, she has become closer to Zoe. As a matter of fact, CJ and Zoe just went to the mall and bought friendship rings. CJ worries what will happen when Morgan finds out. She is right to worry, because Morgan is very hurt. This is just one of the problems that CJ faces this year. She is confused about friendships and about life in general. Why is her life turning upside down? Before this year, everything was simple: ballet and friends. CJ's mom says it is important that CJ keep up with the ballet lessons and recitals. But CJ wants to play soccer, eat candy, and be friends with different kids. She wants to go with the class on field trips instead of going to ballet. CJ is not the same girl she used to be. What's going on?

Learning Extension Ideas

1. Many students face problems similar to CJ's as they go through middle school and on to high school. Things that are important one day just don't seem important the next. Friends may change and goals may change. Have students write about something or someone that was once important to them but isn't any longer. Why have their feelings changed? What activity or person has replaced the old passions?

2. Have students create a scrapbook for CJ or another character from the book. They should include photographs, letters, postcards, keepsake items, newspaper clippings, notes from friends, or anything else they can think of. Have them tell why these items are important to the character.

3. Have students create a program for one of CJ's ballet performances. Ask them: What kind of information is included on a performance program?

4. Ask students: How is the life of a dancer similar to that of an athlete? What do they have in common? What is different?

Booktalk

Yep, Laurence. *Ribbons.* New York: Putnam & Grosset, 1997. IL 5–8, RL 6.7

Robin loves ballet. It means everything to her. It is her whole life. After years of studying, she finally gets to go *en pointe*, to dance on her toes in beautiful ballet shoes. She's excited, ecstatic, she can't wait to learn from her instructor, Madame Oblamov. But wait. Her parents are telling her she has to give up ballet! Give up ballet? She'd just as soon give up breathing. It's not because her parents don't like ballet. It's just that her parents can't afford to pay for the lessons anymore—not if they bring Robin's grandmother to America from China. It costs lots of money to bring someone over. Robin is devastated. How can she love the grandmother who has robbed her of ballet? Will Robin have to give up dance forever?

Learning Extension Ideas

1. Ask students: What does Robin find out about her grandmother? Research the custom that was applied to the grandmother. Why was it started? Has it stopped, or is it still practiced today?

2. If possible, have students attend a ballet, or ask if they have ever seen a ballet. Ask them how the ballet made them feel. Did they understand what was going on?

3. Ask students: If you were trying to describe ballet to someone who knew nothing about it, what would you say? Put yourself in the position of the ballet expert. Tell as much as you can. You will probably need to do some research on the topic!

Suggested Further Reading

Avi. *"Who Was That Masked Man, Anyway?"* New York: Orchard Books, ©1992. IL 5–8, RL 6.3

In the early forties when nearly everyone else is thinking about World War II, sixth-grader Frankie Wattleson gets in trouble at home and at school because of his preoccupation with his favorite radio programs.

Cheaney, J. B. *The Playmaker.* New York: Alfred A. Knopf; distributed by Random House, ©2000. IL 5–8, RL 6.7

While working as an apprentice in a London theater company in 1597, 14-year-old Richard uncovers a mystery involving the disappearance of his father and a traitorous plot to overthrow Queen Elizabeth.

Haas, Jessie. *Will You, Won't You?* New York: Greenwillow Books, ©2000. IL 5–8, RL 6.5

Spending the summer with her strong-willed politician grandmother, 14-year-old Mad achieves breakthroughs in both her horseback riding and her Scottish dancing and begins to develop the self-confidence she has always lacked.

Harrison, Barbara. *Theo.* New York: Clarion Books, ©1999. IL 5–8, RL 8.0

A 12-year-old puppeteer performs bravely on and off the stage after joining the Greek resistance movement during World War II.

Hoobler, Dorothy. *The First Decade: Curtain Going Up.* Brookfield, Conn.: Millbrook Press, ©2000. IL 3–6, RL 4.2

In the early years of the twentieth century, Peggy and her cousins Harry and Jack experience the excitement of belonging to a family of famous actors as they prepare to open a new theater with a family production of an original play.

Horowitz, Anthony. *The Devil and His Boy.* New York: Philomel Books, 2000. IL 5–8, RL 5.3

In 1593, 13-year-old Tom travels through the English countryside to London, where he falls in with a troupe of actors and finds himself in great danger from several sources.

Levy, Elizabeth. *Seventh-Grade Tango.* New York: Hyperion Books for Children, ©2000. IL 5–8, RL 5.8

When Rebecca, a seventh-grader, is paired up with her friend Scott for a dance class at school, she learns a lot about who her real friends are.

Strasser, Todd. *Help! I'm Trapped in a Movie Star's Body.* New York: Scholastic, ©1998. IL 5–8, RL 4.8

Jake switches bodies with Erie Lake, a famous movie star, but eventually Lake gets jealous of Jake for acting too well.

Streatfeild, Noel. *Theater Shoes.* New York: Bullseye Books, 1994, ©1973. IL 5–8, RL 6.5

During World War II in England, three motherless children, whose father is reported missing in action, go to live with their grandmother in London. There they join the members of their talented theatrical family in a school for stage training.

Walton, Darwin McBeth. *Dance, Kayla!* Morton Grove, Ill.: Whitman, 1998. IL 5–8, RL 4.8

Brown-skinned, green-eyed Kayla uses her dancing to help deal with her plight when her grandmother's death and the continued absence of her dancer father make it necessary for her to leave her farm and live in Chicago with relatives.

9 ⁂ Physical Education and Sports

Introduction

Taking physical education classes in the middle school helps students develop positive attitudes toward participation in physical activity. Not all students can become star athletes, but they can learn how to keep fit and active throughout their lives. Students can experience a variety of physical activities and find out for themselves which fit their interests and abilities. They can discover their own aptitudes and preferences for different activities and make informed decisions about the importance of exercise in their lives. It is hoped that all students will develop positive attitudes toward physical activities.

Children love reading about kids their age playing the sports they love. Not everyone is a natural born athlete; not everyone can make the team. But we all should try. This chapter looks at sports stories: some humorous and some serious. The books are grouped by specific sports. Included are classroom activities that deal with sports and the people who play them.

Baseball

Booktalk

Gutman, Dan. *Honus and Me: A Baseball Card Adventure.* New York: Avon Books, 1997. IL 5–8, RL 3.5

Do you love a particular sport, but just aren't as good as the other players? Then you know how Joe Stoshack feels. He just loves baseball, but he doesn't play very well. He can strike out, but that certainly isn't the point of baseball! Then one day as he is helping a neighbor clean out his attic, Joe comes upon

---

RL = Reading Level   *IL = Interest Level*

a baseball card. Not just any baseball card; it's a T-206 Honus Wagner baseball card. The most valuable card in the world! If Joe sells the card, he will be rich! But the card is more valuable than Joe can imagine. You see, the card is magic! It allows Joe to time travel! Joe goes back in time and meets Honus Wagner and gets to attend a World Series game. He also learns a bit about baseball and life in general. Find out how Honus Wagner changes Joe's life.

Learning Extension Ideas

1. Have students work in groups to research a baseball legend. Have them create an imaginary interview with the person that will help the class learn about the life and career of the player.

2. Have students research the history of the World Series. Ask them: When was the first World Series played? Where? What teams were involved, and who won? Have students work in groups. Each group will pick a different World Series to research. Students can prepare PowerPoint presentations about their World Series to present to the class.

Booktalk

Shaughnessy, Dan, and Stan Grossfeld. *Fenway: A Biography in Words and Pictures.* Boston: Houghton Mifflin, 1999. IL YA (Nonfiction)

Fenway Park is the oldest existing baseball park in the United States, and one of the most popular. The Boston Red Sox first played in Fenway Park on April 20, 1912. That was before the *Titanic* sank in the North Atlantic! Before Fenway opened, the Red Sox played at the Huntington Grounds. But in 1912, the Red Sox moved to their new home, and they celebrated by winning the American League Pennant. Why does everyone love Fenway Park? Check out the photographs of this beautiful stadium and meet the players who called it home. There are also interviews with some of the fans who know Fenway. Find out what all the fuss is about. But wait—have you heard? There are now plans to renovate Fenway Park or tear it down and build a new ballpark that will be able to hold more fans. Read all about the oldest existing ballpark in the country in *Fenway: A Biography in Words and Pictures.*

Learning Extension Ideas

1. Talks are underway about replacing Fenway Park with a modern stadium. Have students debate this issue. Should the park be replaced? Renovated? Left alone?

2. Have students design a new baseball stadium. What amenities should it have? For the players? For the fans?

Booktalk

Wolff, Virginia Euwer. *Bat 6.* New York: Scholastic, 1998. IL 5–8, RL 4.8

What would you do if you had two neighboring towns and the residents wouldn't speak to each other? Well, back in 1899, the women in the towns decided to get together and play baseball! While the women played, the men eventually began to talk. This is the fiftieth anniversary of the Barlow–Bear Creek sixth-grade girls' baseball game. The game has evolved into a culminating event for the elementary school. In seventh grade, the girls will be going to school together at the Consolidated School, so this is a good time for the families to get together to enjoy the day. What the towns cannot know is how these girls will change them forever. Join the girls from Barlow and Bear Creek Ridge as they spend their sixth-grade lives getting ready for the big game.

Learning Extension Ideas

1. Bat 6 was begun many years before this particular game was played. Ask students: Why was the game started? Do you think it had been serving its purpose?

2. This story is told in 21 different voices. Ask students: How does this affect the story? Do you find it confusing or helpful for each of the characters to get a chance to tell part of the story?

3. Have students write a paragraph about a sports event. Then have them rewrite it from the perspective of another character. If time allows, have them rewrite it from a third perspective. Ask students: What does this do for the understanding of the paragraph? Does it add to it? Take away from it? Make it clearer to the reader?

Basketball

Booktalk

Moore, Elaine. *Who Let Girls in the Boys' Locker Room?* New York: Troll, 1994. IL 5–8

Michelle is crazy about basketball. She has Michael Jordan posters in her room, she plays on the community basketball team, and she can't wait for junior high when she can be on the school girl's team. Unfortunately, the school budget is slashed and the girl's team is cut. Then the school decides to allow girls on the boys' team. Michelle is one of three girls who make the team. Although the coach welcomes the girls, the boys do not. Will Michelle,

Skye, and Keisha be able to play in spite of the boys? What can they do to make the boys understand that they want to play just as badly as the boys do? Will the boys' stubbornness cost them the big game?

Learning Extension Ideas

1. Federal Title IX law governs the overall equity of treatment and opportunity in athletics while giving schools the flexibility to choose sports based on student body interest, geographic influence, a given school's budget restraints, and gender ratio. In other words, it is not a matter of women being able to participate in wrestling or that exactly the same amount of money is spent on women's and men's basketball. Instead, the focus is on the necessity for women to have equal opportunities to men on a whole, not on an individual basis. Ask students: In light of this federal rule, do you think girls should be allowed on boys' teams? Why or why not?

2. Ask students: On the other hand, should boys be allowed on girls' teams? Why or why not?

3. Ask students: In which sports do you feel boys and girls can compete on an equal basis?

Football

Booktalk

Bissinger, H. G. *Friday Night Lights.* Cambridge: De Capo Press, 2000. IL YA (Nonfiction)

Do any of you play football? Are you on a team, or do you just play with friends? If you are on a team, does your coach talk about winning all the time? Do your parents? In Odessa, Texas, football is everything. There is nothing more in the town. If it weren't for the football team, the town would have disappeared long ago. This book is not fiction. It's a true story about a real town and a real team. The author had heard tales of the Perminan Panthers from Odessa and went to the town to find out about them. Bissinger tells us the story of the football team. We learn more, though. We learn about the lives of the players. We learn about their fathers, brothers, and uncles who played before them. We learn about a town obsessed with the *Friday Night Lights*.

Learning Extension Ideas

1. There is no doubt that football plays a major role in the lives of everyone in Odessa. It may be that there is little else to do in the town. It may also be that the team has been so successful that the town expects it. Ask students to look at the town they live in. Ask them: What is your town known for? What do the residents hold in high esteem? Is it sports? Theater? Or something else?

2. Many Web pages are devoted to following the careers of the players in this book. Have students pick a player and write what might have happened to that person. Then have them research the player on the Internet and see how close the two accounts are.

Hockey

Booktalk

Korman, Gordon. *The Chicken Doesn't Skate.* New York: Scholastic, 1996. IL 5–8, RL 5.5

Ah, the dreaded school science project. How many of us really look forward to that? Most of the kids in this school didn't. Mrs. Bag's sixth-grade class must come up with ideas by the end of the week. When Milo Neal said he was going to do a project on "The Complete Life Cycle of a Link in the Food Chain," Mrs. Bag was delighted. After all, Milo was the son of a famous scientist, so this project had the potential to be really special. She was really looking forward to what fantastic project Milo would come up with. When Milo brings his project to school, the class goes wild. Milo intends to raise a chicken to adulthood right in the classroom. Everyone in the class falls in love with Henrietta the chicken, and they fight for the opportunity to care for her. But how does a science project get involved with the school's hockey team? Find out how one small chicken turns a town upside down in *The Chicken Doesn't Skate.*

Learning Extension Ideas

1. Have students find out about their school's team mascot. Ask them: What is it? Why was it chosen? Do you think it is an appropriate mascot for the school?

2. If your school does not have a team mascot, ask the students what they think it should be. Have students research your school's history and find out what would be a relevant mascot for your school. They should create illustrations showing what the mascot will look like. Have them present the information to the administration and try to have the mascot be adopted by the school.

Soccer

Booktalk

Bloor, Edward. *Tangerine.* San Diego: Harcourt Brace, 1997. IL YA, RL 5.4

How does it feel to be the younger brother of a star athlete? Well, for Paul Fisher, it isn't easy. Paul is visually impaired. This happened when he was five years old. He had an accident that keeps him from playing his favorite sport, soccer. He convinces his parents that their move to Tangerine, Florida, will allow him to play soccer. In spite of his eye problem, he is determined. With the help of special prescription goggles, Paul can see well enough to play. And play he does. It turns out that he is an excellent soccer player. He can also see things that others can't. He sees his older brother as a disturbed young man who has a dangerous side. He sees his father as a man obsessed with Erik's football career. He also sees that Tangerine is a rather odd town. And he starts to remember things that happened when he was five years old. Join the soccer team and find out what is going on in *Tangerine*.

Learning Extension Ideas

1. Have students imagine that they have just been given a job as a real estate agent in Tangerine, Florida. A family with teenaged boys is thinking of moving into the town. What parts of the town would they show the prospective buyers? What would they tell them about what their boys will find? Should they tell the truth or gloss over some of the stranger things about Tangerine?

2. Paul is described as having a disability. Ask students: Do you think he had a "disability" or an "ability?" Defend your answer.

Booktalk

Little, Kimberley Griffiths. *Breakaway.* New York: Avon/ Camelot Book, 1998. IL 5–8, RL 5.5

Have you ever wanted to participate in an activity but couldn't because of things that you had no control over? For Luke Espinosa, the dream of playing soccer is out of his reach. He lives in a trailer park with his mother. There is no extra money from his mother's waitressing job. There is no money for Luke to join the soccer team. There is no money to buy a ball and shin guards. He will just have to go on wishing to play. Still he dreams of being a great soccer player. He can't even learn enough to play it now. Then the coach's son challenges Luke to a grudge match. How will Luke be able to defend himself? Join Luke in this fast-paced sports story.

Learning Extension Ideas

1. Ask students: What does it mean to be a winner? Write about a time when you were a winner.

2. Have students create a sports trivia game. The questions can be about soccer or another sport. Have them write each question on one side of an index card and the answer on the back. They should be sure they can verify the answers. Divide the class into two groups and have the two teams compete against each other to see which half is the "Sports Trivia Rulers."

Booktalk

Wallace, Rich. *Shots on Goal.* New York: Alfred A. Knopf, 1997. IL YA, RL 4.4

Coming back from a disastrous soccer season won't be easy. But best friends Bones and Joey give new life to the team, and they just might be able to energize the rest of the team enough to pull it off. But when the team improves, the friendship begins to disintegrate. The boys start competing to be the best on the team. They also start competing off the field for the affections of a young lady. Can they keep the team winning? Can they keep their friendship going?

Learning Extension Ideas

1. Have students create a motivational speech that will push a losing team up the hill to a win. Ask them: What emotions should you draw on? Can you think of some good motivational clichés?

2. Ask students: What is the difference between healthy competition and being too competitive? Can you be a good sport and still be competitive?

Tennis

Booktalk

Karas, Phyllis. *Cry Baby.* New York: Avon Books, 1996. IL YA

Sam's mother wants her to play tennis. After all, it's a family tradition. And it is expected that she will follow in her sister's footsteps. But, at 15, Sam feels she's old enough to make up her own mind about what she wants to do, and she doesn't want to play tennis. She wants to play lacrosse. So she makes the decision on her own. Her mother is terribly upset when she finds out about it. She thinks that Sam is just doing this to hurt her. Sam is angry at her mother for getting pregnant at age 47! How could she do that? To make things worse, Sam discovers that her best friend is suffering from bulimia. Sam wants to stand by Patsy and help. Patsy's life gets worse when her boyfriend decides to leave her. Sam is worried that Patsy might hurt herself. When Sam goes to see Patsy, there is no answer at the door. Where is Patsy? Find out what happens to Sam, Patsy, and Peter as they try to get through their teen years in *Cry Baby*.

Learning Extension Ideas

1. Bulimia is a serious eating disorder. Athletes must maintain good nutrition to be in top form. Have students research sports nutrition, then create a daily menu for an athlete in serious training.

2. Sam needed to choose between two sports. She was good at both but could only play one. Have students write about a favorite sport as either a spectator or participant.

Booktalk

Wells, Rosemary. *When No One Was Looking.* New York: Scholastic, 1991. IL YA, RL 5.0

Kathy is a good tennis player. In fact, she's more than good. She has the ability and talent to go really far. Everyone has a stake in her career: her parents, coach, and others. At this level of play, tennis is no longer a fun sport. It is hard work and major competition. Everyone wants to make it to the top. Follow Kathy as she works hard for what she wants. At this point, there is only one thing standing in Kathy's way, another player who may be better than Kathy. When a terrible accident eliminates the competition, the race is on to find out what happened to the girl. Poor versus rich, honesty versus deceit, kindness versus cruelty, faith in ability versus rigging the contest: All enter into the story that Kathy lives through. Join Kathy and find out what happens *When No One Was Looking*.

Learning Extension Ideas

1. If this story really happened, you can be sure it would be a lead story in the news for days. Have students write a headline that would accompany the story, as well as a slogan for the television coverage.

2. The role of sports in our society seems to be out of control. Have students write a narrative on the role of sports in our society and what that means to children who are playing sports.

Triathlon

Booktalk

Crutcher, Chris. *Ironman.* New York: Greenwillow Books, 1995. IL YA, RL 6.8

Bo Brewster never gives up. Well, almost never. That's because he dreams of becoming the best triathlete. He is not afraid of hard work. He spends most of his spare time riding or swimming or working out. It isn't easy, but Bo thinks it will be worth it. If only he could do well in school. He has a constant battle with Mr. Redmond. Mr. Redmond is his teacher and is also the football coach. Bo quit football after the coach embarrassed him in front of everyone. Now Mr. Redmond has it in for Bo. When Bo calls Mr. Redmond a bad name, Bo is suspended one more time. Now Bo can't go back to school unless he joins the school anger management class. Bo doesn't want to hang around with the weirdoes in that group, and it will take away time from his training. He is also having trouble with an older kid at the swimming pool who is jealous of Bo because he is a much better swimmer. Things keep getting worse for Bo, but finally he gets the opportunity to compete in a triathlon. He must work harder than ever to compete with the college students who are also entering the contest. Can Bo pull it off? Will he be able to learn to control his anger and concentrate on his training? Who will win the triathlon?

Learning Extension Ideas

1. Throughout the book, Bo writes to Larry King. He believes that once he becomes a famous athlete, he will be a guest on the show. Have students create an interview between Larry King and Bo Brewster. They should invite a few of the other characters from the book to be guests talking about Bo and write a script.

2. Bo has a major problem controlling his anger. Yet he is very much under control when it comes to his training. Ask students: How could Bo use his sports discipline to help him control the rest of his life? What lesson did Bo learn at the end of the book?

Wrestling

Booktalk

Spinelli, Jerry. *There's a Girl in My Hammerlock.* New York: Aladdin, 1993. IL 5–8, RL 5.5

A girl on the boys' wrestling team? It is absolutely unheard of! Who would even imagine something like that? Why would eighth-grader Maisie Potter ever think of such a thing? But Maisie has her reasons for wanting to be on the team. The coach isn't as enthusiastic as others are about the prospect of having a girl on his squad. Some of the boys are openly hostile to Maisie. But Maisie is not a quitter. She works really hard to win a place on the team. Will the boys ever really accept her? Why does she want to be on the team? Will she make her mark?

Learning Extension Ideas

1. Ask students: Why would a girl want to play on a boy's sports team? How do you feel about it? Is there a sport where girls and boys can compete as equals? What is it?

2. Professional wrestling has become quite popular in the past few years. Ask students: How does WWE differ from school wrestling? Which is a truer form of the sport? Why do you think the WWE has become so popular?

Booktalk

Wallace, Rich. *Wrestling Sturbridge.* New York: Alfred A. Knopf, 1996. IL YA, RL 6.0

The thought of spending the rest of his life in Sturbridge is something Ben can't stand. And he certainly doesn't want to go to work in the cinder block factory after graduation. Ben needs a way out of this town. If he stays here, he'll go crazy. Then Ben sees a way out. If he can win the state wrestling championship, maybe he has a chance as a professional wrestler. His best friend is the team's best hope for the championship, but Ben is determined to work hard to win it for himself. Can a small town rivalry crop up between these good friends? Will Ben sacrifice his friendship for his dream? Can Ben ever escape the town he so desperately wants to leave behind?

Learning Extension Ideas

1. All too often, teens pin their future hopes on an unrealistic goal. There are so many teens who think they can make it to the big leagues and escape what life is offering them now. Ask students: Just how realistic is it for a teen to hope to become a professional athlete? Take a major league sport and find out how many athletes are employed. Can students find out what are the odds of a high school player making the team?

2. Ask students: What should a teen do to prepare for a professional sports career? Besides talent, what else is needed? Talk to your local school coaches to get their advice.

Girls' Sports

Booktalk

Macy, Sue. *Girls Got Game: Sports Stories & Poems.* New York: Henry Holt, 2001. IL 5–8, RL 6.5 (Nonfiction)

Girls can play everything from stickball to football, from tetherball to horseback riding. Read 18 stories and poems about girls at their best: girls dealing with gender bias, overcoming fear, and staying competitive. These girls are strong, independent women with the will to succeed. Each story and poem is accompanied by a short biography of the author that highlights her athletic accomplishments. If you enjoy reading about sports, give *Girls Got Game* a read.

Learning Extension Ideas

1. Tell students to write their own stories about experiences they have had in sports. The stories can be about a time they were successful but can also be about a time they failed but learned from the experience. They should be sure to include information about how the event influenced them.

2. Have students create an acrostic poem about a sport. For example:

> **T** he
> **E** vening
> **N** oise of the tennis ball
> **N** ever
> **I** s
> **S** ilent

Suggested Further Reading

Adler, C. S. *Winning.* New York: Clarion Books, ©1999. IL 5–8, RL 6.0

Vicky is thrilled to be on the eighth-grade tennis team, until she realizes that her new playing partner Brenda is ruthless about winning and will even cheat to do so.

Christopher, Matt. *Baseball Turnaround.* Boston: Little, Brown, ©1997. IL 5–8, RL 5.9

Sandy is drawn unknowingly into a shoplifting incident, but his community service involves his beloved baseball. Through his service, he meets people who help him finally put the past behind him.

Crutcher, Chris. *Whale Talk.* New York: Greenwillow Books, ©2001. IL YA, RL 7.0

Intellectually and athletically gifted, TJ, a multiracial, adopted teenager, shuns organized sports and the gung-ho athletes at his high school. Then he agrees to form a swimming team and recruits some of the school's less-popular students.

Gutman, Dan. *Babe and Me: A Baseball Card Adventure.* New York: Avon Books, ©2000. IL 5–8, RL 5.2

With their ability to travel through time using vintage baseball cards, Joe and his father have the opportunity to find out whether Babe Ruth really did call his shot when he hit that home run in the third game of the 1932 World Series against the Chicago Cubs.

Hawk, Tony. *Hawk: Occupation: Skateboarder.* New York: Regan Books, ©2000. IL YA

Internationally known American skateboarding champ Tony Hawk chronicles his life and his very eventful involvement with the sport.

Johnson, Scott. *Safe at Second.* New York: Philomel, ©1999. IL 5–8, RL 7.8

Paulie Lockwood's best friend Todd Bannister is destined for the major leagues until a line drive to the head causes him to lose an eye. They both must find a new future for themselves.

Lynch, Chris. *Gold Dust.* New York: HarperCollins, ©2000. IL 5–8, RL 6.2

In 1975, 12-year-old Richard befriends Napolean, a Caribbean newcomer to his Catholic school. He hopes that Napolean will learn to love baseball and the Red Sox and will win acceptance in the racially polarized Boston school.

Soto, Gary. *Taking Sides.* San Diego: Harcourt Brace, ©1991. IL 5–8, RL 5.7

Fourteen-year-old Lincoln Mendoza, an aspiring basketball player, must come to terms with his divided loyalties when he moves from the Hispanic inner city to a white suburban neighborhood.

Strasser, Todd. *How I Changed My Life.* New York: Aladdin, 1996. IL 5–8, RL 6.4

Overweight high school senior Bo decides to change her image while working on the school play with a former star football player who is also struggling to find a new identity for himself.

Wunderli, Stephen. *The Heartbeat of Halftime.* New York: Henry Holt, 1996. IL 5–8, RL 6.8

Thirteen-year-old Wing clings to the dream that his perpetually losing football team can ride an unexpected winning streak to the championship game before his father dies of cancer.

10 ⨎ Critical Thinking

Introduction

In 1956, Benjamin Bloom headed a group of educational psychologists who developed a classification of levels of intellectual behavior important in learning. Bloom found that more than 95 percent of the test questions students encounter require them to think only at the lowest possible level, the recall of information. As educators, we want our students to go beyond the basic type of learning. We want them to understand what they learn and be able to build on current knowledge. Bloom identified six levels of cognition, which brought the knowledge from simple recall through increasingly more complex and abstract levels to evaluation, the highest level of learning.

Fiction books can be used to teach critical thinking skills as well. Using Bloom's taxonomy, each of these books is shown bringing students through the stages of critical thinking. All levels of Bloom's taxonomy are used for each book.

Booktalk

Alexander, Lloyd. *The Gawgon and the Boy.* New York: Dutton Children's Books, 2001. IL 5–8, RL 5.9

David was not too concerned about his illness. He didn't understand how sick he was, so he wasn't really worried. All he could think about was his good luck at not having to go to school! By May, he had almost recovered, but the doctor told his parents not to risk sending him to school. As a matter of fact, he said it would be a good idea for David to take all next year off as well to keep him from having a relapse. Isn't this every kid's dream? Unfortunately, David's parents decide that he needed a tutor. Boo! David thought he was lucky to get out of school, but now school's coming to him! What's even worse is that Aunt Annie is going to be his tutor. Aunt Annie isn't really his aunt;

RL = Reading Level   *IL = Interest Level*

she lives in the boarding house his grandmother runs and has been a part of the family for years. Annie is old—and scary! David hates the thought of spending each day with Aunt Annie. Why is this happening to him? And what is the Gawgon he keeps seeing?

Learning Extension Ideas

Knowledge

1. Have the students do a quickwrite on what they know about the Great Depression.

Comprehension

2. Have students explain what they think caused the Great Depression. Who was affected? How did it change the lives of ordinary citizens? What was the impact of it?

Application

3. Ask students: Why do you think David kept seeing the Gawgon? Why did it change?

Analysis

4. Ask students: How was the stock market plunge in 1929 different from the October 1987 crash?

Synthesis

5. Throughout the book, David's imagination carried him away. He took pieces of information that he had acquired and wove them into a story, often with humorous results. Have students rewrite the ending of this book as David might have.

Evaluation

6. Have students imagine they are working as a book editor for a large company. Tell them: The manuscript for this book has arrived on your desk. Your job is to tell the author what you think is good and bad about the book. Tell him why you liked certain things and why you didn't like others. Give him any suggestions you may have for changes that you think will make the story more interesting. Use examples from the book to make your point.

Booktalk

Bunting, Eve. *Blackwater.* New York: Joanna Cotler Books, 1999. IL 5–8, RL 5.0

Have you ever done something you know is wrong? Something that you are really ashamed of? Something you wish you could forget? Did you tell anyone about it? Maybe a friend? Maybe a parent? If not, how did it make you feel having to hide what happened? Hiding the truth, but afraid it might sneak out at anytime? Thirteen-year-old Brodie knows what that feels like. He was involved with a very serious event down by the lake. The only witness is his cousin Alex, who wants Brodie to shut up about it. Alex convinces Brodie to just keep his mouth shut and it will all go away. No one ever has to find out. Day after day, the secret eats away at Brodie. He lives in fear. What if the secret gets out? Maybe that would be better. Maybe he should just tell what happened. But what about the consequences that may arise from what happened? Is Brodie ready to face them?

Learning Extension Ideas

Knowledge

1. Have students name the main characters in the book. Ask them: How are they related to each other?

Comprehension

2. Have students describe what happened on the raft. Ask them: Who was involved?

Application

3. Have students come up with a list of rules for water safety. Ask them: What could these teens have done to be safer on the water?

Analysis

4. Ask students: Why do you think Alex told Brodie not to tell the police what happened? Why do you think the other witness kept quiet?

Synthesis

5. Have students rewrite the story as if Brodie had gone to the police immediately after the accident.

Evaluation

6. Ask students: What events could have changed the outcome of this book? Should Brodie have kept quiet, or should he have gone to the police right away? Do you agree with the statement that it is better to tell the truth and face the consequences than to try to cover up?

Booktalk

Carbone, Elisa Lynn. *Storm Warriors.* New York: Alfred A. Knopf, 2001. IL 5–8, RL 6.5

Have you ever heard the term "surfman?" What does the term conjure up in your mind? Back in 1895 off the coast of North Carolina, the surfmen were a brave group of men who worked the Pea Island Life-Saving Station. Their motto was, "You have to go out, but you don't have to come back." Their job was to rescue the crew of ships that had broken up off the coast. Young Nathan Williams lived in a cabin near the Station. He lived with his father and grandfather, who made their living fishing. Nathan loved to watch the surfmen during their drills and even had hopes of one day becoming a surfman himself. But his father was adamantly against the idea. He said Nathan should set his sights on becoming a fisherman and forget about the surfmen. After all, Pea Island has the distinction of being the only African-American Life-Saving crew. No other Station would hire African Americans. And as they retire or leave the service, only their sons or nephews will be hired. There would be no job for Nathan. What should he do? Should he give up his dreams of becoming a surfman? This book is based on the real life adventures of the Pea Island Life-Saving Station in North Carolina. To share some of their incredible rescues and find out what becomes of Nathan, read *Storm Warriors*.

Learning Extension Ideas

Knowledge

1. Ask students: What are the names of the crew of the Pea Island Life-Saving Station?

Comprehension

2. Have students discuss some of the events that caused ships to get into trouble. Ask them: Was it only storms that pressed the Pea Island crew into action?

Application

3. Have students write as many questions with no definitive answer as possible. Questions should relate to the events in the novel.

Analysis

4. Have students explain what type of training would be needed for the crew of Pea Island Station. Tell them: Don't limit your thinking to what is done in the water to rescue sailors. What other training would they need?

Synthesis

5. Ask students: How does the Life-Saving crew compare to today's Coast Guard? How are they the same? How are they different?

Evaluation

6. The area that contained the Pea Island Station is now part of a National Historical Site. Have students take on the role of a tour guide giving tours of the station. Ask them: What would you tell people who visit the site? Why is the site historically important? How would you explain what went on at Pea Island? What characters from the story would you think about including? What stories would you choose to tell? Create a script for your presentation.

Booktalk

Giff, Patricia Reilly. *Nory Ryan's Song.* New York: Delacorte Press, 2000. IL 5–8, RL 5.5

Life is hard in Ireland in 1845. It is not easy being a young Irish girl living during a time when the country is occupied by the British. Wealthy English lords have taken control of the land that once belonged to the Irish. The lords would rather use the land to raise sheep than to grow crops. Nory lives in the West of Ireland with her family. They don't have much money and worry about getting by. Her father is off on a fishing trip trying to raise the money for the rent. Nory's older sister has left the village to emigrate to America. Many young Irish citizens believe they will find their fortune across the wide Atlantic. The departure of Nory's sister means one less mouth to feed, but it also means one less person to work for the family. The potato crop needs to be tended so the family can eat. Soon after Nory's sister leaves, the unthinkable happens. A vicious blight poisons the potato crop. With no means to pay the rent, the family must give up their chickens. Now they have no food supply. Nory must find a way to keep her family from starving to death. How much is she willing to risk to save the lives of her family? Will she succeed?

Learning Extension Ideas

Knowledge

1. Have students do a quickwrite about the Irish famine. Ask them: What do you know about that time in history? In what years did it occur? Did it affect everyone in Ireland?

Comprehension

2. Have students explain why the Irish lived mostly on potatoes. Ask them: Why was there so little other food available? Why didn't they plant other crops, instead of depending on one?

Application

3. Ask students: What could have been done to help the poor of Ireland? Why was so little done?

Analysis

4. Ask students: Are there other parts of the world where famine is a problem? What steps are being taken to help the victims?

Synthesis

5. The Irish are portrayed as very superstitious people. Have students research Irish superstitions and make a chart of them. Ask them: How many have you heard of? Are these superstitions still held today?

Evaluation

6. The ships that the Irish took to America were nicknamed the "coffin ships." Conditions on the ships were horrible, but the dream of life in a new country kept the immigrants going. Have students write an ending to the story that tells what Nory found when she reached America. Ask them: Will she find her family? Will she go to school or get a job? Where will she settle?

Booktalk

Hesser, Terry Spencer. *Kissing Doorknobs.* New York: Delacorte Press, 1998. IL YA, RL 5.8

Tara can't stop to answer her friends' questions. She must keep counting the cracks on the sidewalk. When she is interrupted, she must go home and start all over again. She doesn't understand why she needs to count. All she knows is that she can't stop. Something happened when she heard, "Step on a crack, you'll break your mother's back." Now Tara must also be sure not to step on cracks as she counts on her way to school. She also must pray. Tara knows this annoys her family and friends, but she can't help herself. As the years go by, her rituals become more bizarre and more disturbing to her family. What is wrong with Tara? Can she be helped?

Learning Extension Ideas

Knowledge

1. Have students list the characters in the book. Ask them: What is their relationship to each other?

Comprehension

2. Ask students: What are some of the symptoms of obsessive-compulsive-disorder (OCD)?

Application

3. Have students research OCD. Ask them: What are the causes? What are the treatments?

Analysis

4. Have students explain the causes of OCD. Ask them: Is it an easily recognized disorder?

Synthesis

5. Ask students: How does OCD interfere with a person's life? What ordinary things can be affected? How does it affect the family and friends of the patient?

Evaluation

6. Have students create a magazine issue devoted to OCD. There should be background articles about the illness, reports on research, interviews with those afflicted with the illness, major breakthroughs, and so forth. There can even be advertisements related to things found in the novel and a "Dear Abby" section with letters seeking advice in dealing with OCD. Illustrations can come from the Internet or be drawn by the students. The articles should be typed in columns. The magazine can be constructed using a word processing package and newsletter template or it can be cut and pasted by hand.

Booktalk

Hite, Sid. *Stick and Whittle.* New York: Scholastic, 2000. IL 5–8, RL 6.1

Melvin Fitchett is feeling pretty good about his life. It's 1872, he has survived the Civil War, and he has been living on his own for seven years now. He is foot loose and fancy free. His one regret in life is that he lost the woman he loved. She was told that he died in the war, so she left for good. Melvin heard she signed on as a governess with a family and moved out West. Now Melvin goes in search of his lost love. He knows it isn't likely that he will ever find her, but every man needs a reason to go on. When he comes upon a young boy alone on the prairie, he lets the boy tag along. Incredibly, the boy's name is also Melvin. To avoid confusion they give each other nicknames—Stick and Whittle. Stick is big Melvin and Whittle is little Melvin. Together they share many adventures as they ride the prairie. Will Stick find his true love? Will Whittle do the world a favor? And what secrets are these two hiding from the world?

Learning Extension Ideas

Knowledge

1. Have students describe the setting of this novel. Ask them: When and where does it take place?

Comprehension

2. Have students discuss what life was like for these two men. Ask them: Did they have family? Did they have a home? Where were they heading?

Application

3. Whittle describes his journey from Chicago to the time he meets up with Stick. Have students draw a map that shows his journey.

Analysis

4. Whittle talks of "man infested destiny." Stick corrects him and tries to explain the concept to him. Ask students: What was Stick talking about, and how does it fit into the story line?

Synthesis

5. Stick and Whittle talk about the disappearing buffalo on the American Plains. Ask students: What happened to the buffalo? How did it happen? What steps have been taken to bring the buffalo back? Have they been successful?

Evaluation

6. Stick loved to read the newspaper. In fact, that is where he got a very important clue to finding his long-lost love. Have students create a newspaper that Stick may have read. The newspaper should be word processed and typed in columns. Students should be sure to include a variety of news articles. It may also include advertisements, obituaries, editorials, personal ads, or anything else that may have appeared in 1872. Articles should have headlines and bylines. All material should be appropriate for the time period and should be relevant to the novel.

Booktalk

Lawrence, Iain. *The Wreckers.* New York: Delacorte Press, 1998. IL 5–8, RL 4.2

In the year 1799, young John Spencer is aboard his father's shipping vessel off the coast of Cornwall. It's the first time he's been allowed to journey with his father. What a great way to see the world. They've visited Greece, Italy, and Spain. Now they're heading home. Things are going well until a large storm hits in the night. They are sure they will be lost at sea. But then they see signal lights coming from the shore. The sailors are wary of the signal lights. Are they lights from friendly folk trying to help guide them in, or are they the lights of the wreckers? Wreckers were notorious for guiding ships onto the rocks to be smashed and destroyed. Then the wreckers could scavenge the contents of the ship and kill the crew. In 1799, there are communities along the coast of Cornwall that are totally dependent on this livelihood. What will happen to the ship? What will happen to John? Are they being guided by friendly villagers or the notorious *Wreckers*?

Learning Extension Ideas

Knowledge

1. Have students list the characters in the book. Ask them: What is their relationship to each other?

Comprehension

2. Have students summarize the plot of the book. Ask them: What are the major events?

Application

3. Ask students: What was the purpose of the wreckers? Was it really possible for a village to survive using this method? What types of cargo were carried on the ships?

Analysis

4. Ask students: Did all the villagers take part in this practice? How did they feel about this practice?

Synthesis

5. Ask students: Are there any modern wreckers? How is this practiced in today's society?

Evaluation

6. Have students imagine that Ricki Lake has called. She wants to interview the characters in this book. She wants to get both sides of the story. She thinks the villagers have gotten a bad rap and she wants to give them a chance to defend themselves on national television. Students can work in groups to script the show. The show should have the feeling of a "live" show that is not following a script, but there should be a script that can be turned in. The show should include a catchy theme song. Assign roles of the characters in the book and Ricki Lake to students. Other students can be part of the audience. Introduce each character and explain how they fit into the show. The characters should be asked probing questions that get to the heart of the topic. Explore their motivations and beliefs. Try to have them see the other side of the argument. Audience members should be included as well. They can ask questions or offer comments. Be sure to include at least one well-timed commercial break in the show that is related to the novel.

Booktalk

Mazer, Harry. *A Boy at War: A Novel of Pearl Harbor.* New York: Simon & Schuster Books for Young Readers, 2001. IL 5–8, RL 8.5

Adam is starting out at yet another school. Being the child of a military man has its problems. The family moves around so much that it seems like Adam is always starting in a new school. This one is different. For the first time, he is attending a civilian school instead of a military base school. And this is the first time he's lived in Hawaii. The Hawaiian kids don't seem to want to hang around with a white kid from New York. Then Davi, a young Japanese-American boy, befriends Adam and they start hanging out together. The year is 1941, and there is political tension between the United States and Japan. There are even rumors that Japan wants to go to war with the United States. Adam's father demands that he stop hanging around with Davi. It just doesn't look right to be associating with a Japanese boy. Adam disobeys his father and sneaks out to go fishing with Davi and his friend Martin. While they are out in a rowboat in Pearl Harbor, the boys are caught in a massive invasion by the Japanese. The three boys struggle to survive the attack as chaos breaks out all around them. Join Adam on December 7, 1941, a "date that will live in infamy."

Learning Extension Ideas

Knowledge

1. Ask students: What do you know about the attack on Pearl Harbor? Using two columns, compile a list of things you know are true and things you think are true.

Comprehension

2. Have students summarize the events of December 7, 1941. Ask them: How many ships were lost? How many military men? How many civilians?

Application

3. Have students research what life was like for Japanese living on the island after the bombing. Ask them: Were they allowed to stay? If they were taken away as Davi's father was, where were they taken? Were they allowed to return?

Analysis

4. Ask students: Why do you think so many people visit the *Arizona* each year? What does it mean to them? Why do you think the ship was never brought to the surface as the other ships were?

Synthesis

5. Have students work in groups to create a newscast from December 7, 1941. They should be sure to limit their news to what was known at that time and keep in mind that they do not want to give any important information to the Japanese.

Evaluation

6. Students can create hypertext essays explaining what happened on the fateful day of December 7, 1941. Using library print sources, electronic resources, and the Internet, they can gather information and organize it into an understandable format. Students can then write a short hypertext essays about the day. The essays can be typed into a word processing program and then converted to html

format. Have students include five hot links within their essays that point to other sites. The other sites will include:

• Three Internet pages that have appropriate information about what is being discussed in the essay.

• Two links to pages composed by the student. These pages must be appropriate to the essay. Examples of some student-generated pages are a bibliography of books dealing with the topic, a drawing done by the student, and a poem written by the student.

Essays can be uploaded onto the school server or previewed locally from disk. To see examples of hypertext essays, visit http://rms .concord.k12.nh.us/sacks.

Booktalk

Murphy, Jim. *The Great Fire.* New York: Scholastic, 1995. IL 5–8, RL 6.5 (Nonfiction)

Have you ever witnessed a fire? Maybe a building in your town burned as you were passing by. It is a horrible scene. Even if everyone gets out safely, they are faced with the knowledge that their personal property has been destroyed. Years of memories go up in flames. Now imagine what it might be like if there were several buildings on fire. What if the fire keeps spreading out of control? What if the fire lasts days? That is exactly what happened in Chicago. On October 8, 1871, the residents of Chicago were enjoying a warm Sunday evening. There was no indication, no warning of what was to come. Then, in a barn, a small fire started. The owners of the barn had gone to bed early and didn't notice. A friend who stopped by for a visit spotted the fire and unsuccessfully tried to put it out. Through a serious of unfortunate mistakes, the fire spread through the streets of Chicago. The fire continued to burn for three days, until Tuesday, when it was finally extinguished. Two-thirds of the city was destroyed in the fire. But what about the people? What happened to them? Did they escape? Read the story of the *Great Fire*.

Learning Extension Ideas

Knowledge

1. At the beginning of this book, the author introduces us to the main characters of the book. Have students create a chart that lists the characters and their importance to the story.

Comprehension

2. The fire was a result of many factors. Ask students: What conditions existed in Chicago during that time that made it a prime location for a disastrous fire?

Application

3. From the beginning, one mistake after another was made, each contributing to the disaster. Have students chronicle the mistakes and explain why they were errors.

Analysis

4. Ask students: How have firefighting techniques improved since this fire? What modern devices would have prevented this catastrophe?

Synthesis

5. Ask students: What character was most relevant to you? Whose story were you most affected by? Why?

Evaluation

6. Have students create a timeline that explains the important events in this disaster. Events should be organized chronologically. Students can write short descriptions and explanations of the events. They should identify persons involved in the event and add pictures to make the timeline interesting. Further information can be obtained from The Great Chicago Fire Web site, at http://www.chicagohs .org/fire.

Booktalk

Shusterman, Neal. *Downsiders.* New York: Simon & Schuster Books for Young Readers, 1999. IL 5–8, RL 6.4

Have you ever wondered what it's like under the ground that you walk on? Is there life underground? Of course we all know about bugs and worms and creepy crawlies, but is there any other type of life? What if there is a whole world underground? Maybe where we see skyscrapers, they see mountains. What if it is just the downside of our upside? What if there are people living there? Not quite like us, though. Can you picture it? Maybe you have an idea what Downsiders are like. Lindsay has moved into a brownstone apartment with her father and stepbrother. They are renovating the building and have unknowingly left a doorway to the Downside open. Talon climbs up in search of medicine for his younger sister. What will happen when Talon and Lindsey meet? There is a strict law against Downsiders and Topsiders meeting. Will this encounter change the way they live?

Learning Extension Ideas

Knowledge

1. Have students name the major Downsider characters. Ask them: What is their relationship to each other?

Comprehension

2. Have students describe the Talon's home beneath the city.

Application

3. Ask students: How does Lindsay react when she sees the Downside? How do you think you would feel?

Analysis

4. When a construction project threatens to unearth the secret world of the Downsiders, Talon and Lindsay must both decide how to proceed. Ask students: How would you go about deciding which world is more important?

Synthesis

5. The Downsiders describe the Topside life as outsiders would. They don't understand what is going on, so they try to interpret what they see in relationship to what they know. For example, when the Downsider expedition sneaks up a manhole cover during a marathon race, they talk about thousands of people running in an endless pack wearing short pants and numbers on their backs. Many of their descriptions are humorous. Have students write a short story about a common event but from a Downsider's point of view.

Evaluation

6. Have students create their own Downside World. Ask them: What would it look like? What types of people would live there? Would they be like us or totally different? Create a diorama of what your world would look like. Include a map that shows us how to get around. Be sure to also include a drawing of what the inhabitants look like.

Suggested Further Reading

Cummings, Priscilla. *A Face First.* New York: Dutton Children's Books, ©2001. IL 5–8, RL 6.0

Twelve-year-old Kelley decides to cut off contact with her friends and classmates after suffering third-degree burns to her face and body in a car accident near her home on Maryland's Kent Island.

Holt, David. *Spiders in the Hairdo: Modern Urban Legends.* Little Rock, Ark.: August House, ©1999. IL YA, RL 5.4

A collection of urban legends revolving around topics such as college, crime, and jerks.

Holt, Kimberly Willis. *When Zachary Beaver Came to Town.* New York: Henry Holt, 1999. IL 5–8, RL 5.0

During the summer of 1971 in a small Texas town, 13-year-old Toby and his best friend Cal meet the star of a sideshow act, 600-pound Zachary, the fattest boy in the world.

Kindl, Patrice. *Goose Chase.* Boston: Houghton Mifflin, 2001. IL 5–8, RL 6.5

Rather than marry a cruel king or a seemingly dim-witted prince, an enchanted goose girl endures imprisonment, capture by several ogresses, and other dangers, before learning exactly who she is.

Konigsburg, E. L. *The View from Saturday.* New York: Atheneum Books for Young Readers, ©1996. IL 3–6, RL 4.8

Four students, each with his or her own individual story, develop a special bond and attract the attention of their teacher, a paraplegic, who chooses them to represent their sixth-grade class in the Academic Bowl competition.

Lowry, Lois. *The Giver.* Boston: Houghton Mifflin, 1993. IL YA, RL 5.7

Given his lifetime assignment at the Ceremony of Twelve, Jonas becomes the receiver of memories shared by only one other in his community and discovers the terrible truth about the society in which he lives.

Paterson, Katherine. *Lyddie.* New York: Lodestar Books, ©1991. IL 5–8, RL 6.5

An impoverished Vermont farm girl, Lyddie Worthen, is determined to gain her independence by becoming a factory worker in Lowell, Massachusetts, in the 1840s.

Peck, Richard. *A Year Down Yonder.* New York: Dial Books for Young Readers, ©2000. IL 5–8, RL 5.2

During the Depression in 1937, 15-year-old Mary Alice is sent to live with her feisty, larger-than-life grandmother in rural Illinois, and she comes to a better understanding of this fearsome woman.

Wilson, Nancy Hope. *Mountain Pose.* New York: Farrar, Straus & Giroux, 2001. IL 5–8, RL 5.2

When 12-year-old Ellie inherits an old Vermont farm from her cruel and heartless grandmother Aurelia, she reads a set of diaries written by an ancestor and discovers secrets from the past.

Wolff, Virginia Euwer. *Make Lemonade.* New York: Henry Holt, ©1993. IL YA, RL 5.2

To earn money for college, 14-year-old LaVaughn babysits for a teenage mother.

11 ❦ Just for Fun

Introduction

Everyone needs a good laugh now and again. It is said that laughter is the best medicine. During times of crisis, children often enjoy reading humorous stories. They may not be looking for the tear-jerker novels that they read during good times. The ability to laugh at ourselves and the madness of the world is a great gift that makes it easier to be a child. In this chapter you'll find a collection of novels sure to entertain and soften even the worst mood. Students enjoy reading about the funny things that kids do, and you can continue the laughs through the classroom activities.

Another enjoyable yet educational topic for students is holiday celebrations. There is something appealing about holidays. Whether it is a religious holiday like Christmas or a national holiday like Thanksgiving, we all love a celebration. Students are fascinated by holidays, they get excited around holiday times, and they love reading about holidays. In addition to the mainstream holidays celebrated in the United States, students often enjoy hearing about holidays celebrated by others. In this chapter are some wonderful books about holidays, in which students can discover the origins of familiar holidays and learn about some holidays that they may have only just heard of.

This chapter surveys some of the delightful humorous books that have recently been released, as well as books about holidays. Educators may want to use the humorous books as read-alouds, then tie them into classroom activities. The holiday books can be used to teach students about different holidays celebrated around the world and can complement social studies and learning units on specific countries. Of course, all of these titles are enjoyable on their own—and students may wish to read them "just for fun."

Humor

Booktalk

Conford, Ellen. *The Frog Princess of Pelham.* Boston: Little, Brown, 1997. IL 5–8, RL 4.1

Chandler has everything that money can buy. That is, everything but love. Orphaned at age nine, Chandler lives with her cousin, Horace, who is more interested in spending her money than caring for her. Chandler is not looking forward to school vacation week. Horace is off to Switzerland, and he has arranged for Chandler to spend the week at a survival camp in the mountains. Chandler doesn't have many friends in school. She is far from popular, especially with the boys. She thinks it is a dream when Danny Malone asks her for a kiss. And what a kiss it is! Chandler feels she is melting. But that's when the trouble starts. When she opens her eyes, the world looks different. All she can see is Danny's foot. He looks like a giant. And she suddenly has a craving for flies. Is it possible that she has turned into a frog? If so, how can she get back to her old self?

Learning Extension Ideas

1. This tale is a takeoff on a popular fairy tale. Have students choose another fairy tale and retell it as if it was happening today.

2. Have students find other variations of the frog prince story. Ask them: How many can you find? What makes them different?

Booktalk

DiCamillo, Kate. *Because of Winn-Dixie.* Cambridge, Mass.: Candlewick Press, 2000. IL 3–6, RL 5.8

"My name is India Opal Buloni, and last summer my daddy, the preacher, sent me to the store for a box of macaroni-and-cheese, some white rice, and two tomatoes and I came back with a dog." So begins the story of young India and her life in a new town. It's not easy moving to a new town and trying to make friends. When India meets a stray dog, she knows right away that she has found a true friend. She names the dog Winn-Dixie after the supermarket she found him in. Winn-Dixie is big, mangy, and perhaps the ugliest dog India has ever seen. But when he smiles, his whole body smiles. India has never known a dog that could smile, but Winn-Dixie sure can. Suddenly, life becomes more exciting. Join India and Winn-Dixie as they encounter some of the unusual characters in Naomi, Florida. Now it seems to India that every good thing that happens to her happens *Because of Winn-Dixie*.

Learning Extension Ideas

1. Have students create a photo album to illustrate the book. Have the "models" pose with props, costumes, or backgrounds that go along with the story. Once the students have their photos, they should arrange them in an album in the order that the events occurred in the book. Have the students write captions that explain the photos and provide an approximate date. On the inside of the album, they should create an index sheet that explains who the characters are and any other identifying information about them.

2. Have students make a list of 10 things about someone they love and give it to that person as a present.

Booktalk

Fleischman, Sid. *Bo & Mzzz Mad.* New York: HarperCollins, 2001. IL 3–6, RL 3.9

The Gamages and the Martinkas hate each other. The family feud has been going on for a very long time. It started over a gold strike back in the 1800s and has lasted all these years. Bo Gamage has no desire to meet the other side of his family, but he has no choice. Both his parents have died, so his choice is to go live with Paw Paw Martinka or be sent to a foster home. He figures he will meet the Martinkas and then run away. So here he is, being dropped off in the middle of the desert with no one to pick him up. Just like the Martinkas to leave him to die in the heat. But then he sees a Chevy truck the color of day-glo red lipstick. Driving the truck is a girl who looks to be about 13 years old. She is wearing big movie star sunglasses and a billed pink cap that says Mad. This couldn't be his cousin, could it? The girl calls herself Mzzz Mad, and she's about as happy to see Bo and he is to see her. What could these two possibly have in common? Maybe there is a good reason for the family feud.

Learning Extension Ideas

1. Hatred tears families apart, yet is often the easiest path to take. Peace brings benefits to all, yet is the path that requires the most effort on each person's part. Have students write an ending to the story that shows whether the family feud is over.

2. During the 1800s there were lots of prospectors looking for gold in the West. Ask students: Are there any today? Research the question and discuss whether and why there are modern day prospectors.

Booktalk

Haddix, Margaret Peterson. *Just Ella.* New York: Simon & Schuster Books for Young Readers, 1999. IL YA, RL 5.5

You've heard the story of Cinderella, right? Her fairy godmother rescues her from her cruel stepmother, she goes to the ball, meets her prince, and lives happily ever after. You probably think that was the end of the story. But have you ever really thought about it? Maybe things didn't turn out so great for Cinderella. Here's the story of what really happens after the ball. Cinderella is sent to the castle to live until the wedding. She is given lessons on royal deportment. After all, she must learn to be a princess. What she learns is that women are meant to be seen and not heard. And she has nothing to do all day but do needlepoint. So many interesting things are off limits because they are not ladylike. When she is finally allowed to attend a tournament, she finds that she must stay inside a tent. She is not allowed to be in the sun or to watch the tournament. And the prince! How could she have known that he was so dim-witted? In fact, he's incredibly boring! What is a girl to do in this situation? What would you do? Would you stay and marry the prince, or would you try to leave?

Learning Extension Ideas

1. Most versions of the Cinderella story end with her living happily ever after with her Prince Charming. This tale takes over where the others stop. Have the students take well-known fairy tales and create new endings for them (e.g., Snow White, The Three Little Pigs).

2. In the story, an alternative explanation for Cinderella's appearance at the ball is suggested. Ella insists there was no fairy godmother and goes on to explain how she got the glass slippers, the dress, the coach, and so forth. Have students use another well-known fairy tale and provide alternate explanations to what is seen as magic. For instance, maybe Rapunzel actually had a ladder.

Booktalk

Klise, Kate. *Regarding the Fountain.* New York: Avon Books, 1998. IL 5–8, RL 4.8

Dry Creek Middle School needs a new water fountain. The old one is broken and should be replaced. So a letter is sent requesting a proposal from Ms. Florence Waters to replace the water fountain. Ms. Waters asks the fifth grade for input on how the new fountain should look, since they are the ones that will see it the most. This begins a comedy of errors as letters, memos, and postcards flow back and forth—with no one really communicating. Pay attention to the subtle clues along the way. They may just be leading up to a mystery *Regarding the Fountain.*

Learning Extension Ideas

1. This is a funny book about misunderstandings. Words are misinterpreted and changed around. Have your own fun with words by playing a game of fictionary. Give each student an unfamiliar word. Have students use a dictionary to find the correct meaning of their words. They will then create three definitions for each word, only one of which is true. The made-up definitions should be believable. The class will then have a chance to look at all the words and try to guess which definition is accurate.

2. Misunderstandings sometimes happen between people and cause hard feelings. These situations are often brought about by miscommunication. Have students write about a time when they had a misunderstanding with someone. Ask them: How did it feel? How did you go about resolving the situation? How could you have avoided the situation?

Booktalk

Korman, Gordon. *The 6th Grade Nickname Game.* New York: Hyperion, 1998. IL 3–6, RL 4.8

Do you have a nickname? Who gave it to you? Often parents or siblings are the ones to give nicknames. Sometimes it's friends. In this case, it's Wiley and Jeff. They are so good at giving people nicknames that the names stick no matter what. The principal is Deer in Headlights and the kid who is always snooping around is called Snoopy. Wiley and Jeff love to play this game. They can make unpopular kids cool just by giving them good nicknames. It's fun. Until the new girl arrives. They both like her and can't come up with a good nickname for her. They also want to help out a teacher who is in trouble because the students didn't do well on the standardized test. What happens?

Learning Extension Ideas

1. Survey the class. How many have nicknames? What is the meaning behind the nicknames? Who gave the nicknames? Do they like their nicknames? Have students chart the answers. Which percentage of students have nicknames?

2. Have students create nicknames for themselves. They should write a paragraph that states the nickname and why they feel the nickname

suits them, then share the writing with the class. Give them an opportunity to comment on the appropriateness of the nicknames.

Booktalk

Lindsay, Janice. *The Milly Stories: Corpses, Carnations, the Weirdness Index, and, of Course, Aunt Gloria.* New York: DK Publishing, 1998. IL 5–8, RL 6.2

Milly went to live with Aunt Gloria and Uncle Edgar after her mother died. It's
weird to be living in a funeral home, but it leads to some very funny adventures. Can you imagine a Halloween party in a funeral home? But now Aunt
Gloria has died. Milly wonders what will become of her. Maybe she can stay
with her Harley-riding grandmother. On top of that, Milly keeps hearing
voices—like Aunt Gloria's, telling her to behave. Join Milly as she learns to
listen to the voices that matter the most.

Learning Extension Ideas

1. Students can create a paper bag book report. Give each student a
   small paper bag to put items in that relate to Milly and the story.
   The students can use drawings, magazine clippings, real life objects
   (e.g., carnations), and so forth. Then they should tell the class how
   each object relates to the story.

2. Milly suffers several losses in her life. In spite of her pain, she finds
   she can have fun in life and share laughter with friends. Have students
   write about a time in their lives when they were down and explain
   what or who helped lift them up.

Booktalk

Mills, Claudia. *Losers, Inc.* New York: Farrar, Straus & Giroux, 1997. IL 5–8, RL 4.2

Ethan Winfield and Julius Zimmerman think of themselves as sixth-grade
losers. They aren't very good students; they aren't very good athletes. They
aren't really good at much. As a matter of fact, they have created their own
club, Losers, Inc. But things change for Ethan when Ms. Gunderson begins
her student teaching. She's beautiful and seems to think Ethan has more to
offer than he's been showing. Ethan falls totally in love with her. He decides
to work as hard as he can to impress his student teacher. Other kids notice
and begin to tease Ethan. It gets so bad that Ethan takes out his frustration
on one of the girls. Afterward he is much too ashamed to admit what he did,

even to Julius. As he continues to try to impress Ms. Gunderson, Julius is pushed farther away. Will Ethan risk losing his best friend just to impress a teacher?

Learning Extension Ideas

1. Not everyone thinks of himself or herself as a loser. Ask students: If you and your friend were to create a secret club, what would it be called? Create some rules for the club. Would it be exclusive, or would you let others join?

2. Have students take on the role of another friend of Ethan and Julius. What advice would they give Ethan and Julius as they struggle through the events in the story?

Booktalk

Pullman, Philip. *I Was a Rat!* New York: Alfred A. Knopf, 2000. IL 3–6, RL 5.4

The young boy seemed an ordinary enough boy. But the old couple didn't know what to make of him when he told them that he used to be a rat. It's true that his behavior was a bit off. He had a tendency to shred his bedclothes to make a nest. He ate just about anything he could find. And he had no manners to speak of. But the couple were childless and felt a strange attachment to the peculiar little boy. When the Royal Philosopher heard the stories about the rat boy, he took it upon himself to investigate the claim. The old couple couldn't refuse the request that the boy be brought to the castle. Little did they know what chain of events would be triggered by this. Who was the boy, and what will happen to him? Was he really a rat in boy's clothing? And what does the new Princess know about all this?

Learning Extension Ideas

1. Have students rewrite traditional fairy tales from a different angle. They can change the main character or add a different slant to the story. Moving the character by changing location or time period is a great way to rewrite a traditional fairy tale. Students can tell what they think happened to the character after the original story ends.

2. Throughout this book, some of the story is told in newspaper clippings. Have students create a newspaper with all the stories included based on a fairy tale. The students can work in groups. Each newspaper article should be written as if it were a straight news story. The students should be sure to use the five Ws of newspaper reporting.

They can illustrate their "news" stories by drawing on the computer or by hand.

Booktalk

Rennison, Louise. *Angus, Thongs and Full-Frontal Snogging: Confessions of Georgia Nicolson.* New York: Harper-Collins, 2000. IL YA, RL 5.1

Angus, Thongs and Full-Frontal Snogging. Did that get your attention? Well, join Georgia Nicolson, age 14, as she attempts to survive adolescence. Life definitely has its ups and downs for Georgia. For instance, the time she dressed as a stuffed olive at the costume party. And, yes, that was her cat attacking the poodle. Georgia keeps trying to act cool in front of other people, but she often ends up looking ridiculous, especially when she's in front of that gorgeous guy, Robbie. Georgia keeps a running list of the things that are wrong with her life. You'll have a good laugh with Georgia Nicolson in *Angus, Thongs and Full-Frontal Snogging.*

Learning Extension Ideas

1. Read through Georgia's list of six things that are wrong with her life. Have students create their own lists. What can they do to improve their lot? Have them make a list of six things that are good about their lives.

2. We often see ourselves very differently than do those around us. Ask students: Do you think people notice the things you do as much as you do? Write a paragraph on the topic "Am I weird?"

Suggested Further Reading

Anderson, Matthew T. *Burger Wuss.* Cambridge, Mass.: Candlewick Press, 1999. IL YA

Hoping to shake his loser image, Anthony plans revenge on a bully, which results in a war between two competing fast-food restaurants, Burger Queen and O'Dermott's.

Honey, Elizabeth. *Don't Pat the Wombat!* New York: Alfred A. Knopf, 2000, ©1996. IL 5–8, RL 6.5

Wormz, Nicko, and their friends fear that their experience at a school camp in the Australian bush will be ruined by the presence of the dreaded Mr. Cromwell as a substitute chaperon.

Karr, Kathleen. *The Great Turkey Walk.* New York: Farrar, Straus & Giroux, 1998. IL 5–8, RL 4.8

In 1860, a somewhat simple-minded 15-year-old boy attempts to herd 1,000 turkeys from Missouri to Denver, Colorado, in hopes of selling them at a profit.

Klise, Kate. *Letters from Camp.* New York: Avon Books, ©1999. IL 5–8, RL 6.7

Sent to Camp Happy Harmony to learn how to get along with each other, pairs of brothers and sisters chronicle in letters home how they come to suspect the intentions of the singing family running the camp.

Korman, Gordon. *No More Dead Dogs.* New York: Hyperion Books for Children, ©2000. IL 3–6, RL 5.3

Eighth-grade football hero Wallace Wallace is sentenced to detention attending rehearsals of the school play. There, in spite of himself, he becomes wrapped up in the production and begins to suggest changes that improve not only the play but his life as well.

Lynch, Chris. *Extreme Elvin.* New York: HarperCollins, ©1999. IL YA

As he enters high school, 14-year-old Elvin continues to deal with his weight problem as he tries to find his place among his peers.

Paulsen, Gary. *The Schernoff Discoveries.* New York: Delacorte Press, ©1997. IL 5–8, RL 6.0

Harold and his best friend, both hopeless geeks and social misfits, try to survive unusual science experiments, the attacks of the football team, and other dangers of junior high school.

Peck, Richard. *Fair Weather: A Novel.* New York: Dial Books, 2001. IL 5–8, RL 6.3

In 1893, 13-year-old Rosie and members of her family travel from their Illinois farm to Chicago to visit Aunt Euterpe and attend the World's Columbian Exposition, which, along with an encounter with Buffalo Bill and Lillian Russell, turns out to be a life-changing experience for everyone.

Pinkwater, Daniel Manus. *Fat Camp Commandos.* New York: Scholastic, 2001. IL 5–8, RL 7.9

Ralph and Sylvia Nebula and their friend Mavis Goldfarb are bitter about being sent to a bogus weight-loss camp, so they decide to escape and find a way to take revenge on those responsible for promoting the idea that thin is better.

Snicket, Lemony. *The Bad Beginning.* New York: Harper-Collins, ©1999. IL 5–8, RL 6.0

After the sudden death of their parents, the three Baudelaire children must depend on each other and their wits, especially when it turns out that the distant relative who is appointed their guardian is determined to use any means necessary to get their fortune.

Holidays Around the World

Latino Holidays

BOOKTALK

Menard, Valerie. *The Latino Holiday Book: From Cinco De Mayo to Dia de los Muertos: The Celebrations and Traditions of Hispanic-Americans.* New York: Marlowe, 2000. IL AD (Nonfiction)

Have you heard of Cinco de Mayo or Navidad? How about Dia de los Muertos, or Dia de los Reyes? How much do you know about Latino holidays? This book will tell you what you need to know to understand and celebrate the holidays. In addition to telling us what the holiday celebrates, we also learn how to celebrate the correct way. There are even some recipes to try. Let's celebrate the Latino way with the *Latino Holiday Book.*

LEARNING EXTENSION IDEAS

1.   Holidays and celebrations play a major role in most cultures. Have students choose one of the holidays from this book to explore further. Students can create a children's storybook explaining the holiday.

2.   Food is a large part of most celebrations. Have students attempt to make some of the traditional holiday foods.

Valentine's Day

BOOKTALK

Bulla, Clyde Robert. *The Story of Valentine's Day.* New York: HarperCollins, 1999. IL 3–6, RL 6.8 (Nonfiction)

What do you think of when someone says "Valentine's Day?" Cards? Candy? Hearts and flowers? Well, did you know that the holiday actually came from the Roman holiday Lupercalia? It was a great festival that celebrated the coming of spring. After the rise of Christianity in the West, the Roman Catholic Church began to use the festival to honor St. Valentine. But there's more! If you want to find out the true and fascinating facts about St. Valentine's Day, check out this book. You'll find out just who Valentine was, when the holiday became the love holiday, and when the tradition of exchanging cards arose. It's all here.

LEARNING EXTENSION IDEAS

1. This is a great book to read before starting any Valentine's Day project. Have the students create unusual Valentine's cards that include some of the facts surrounding this holiday.

2. Have students create trifolded pamphlets. Each section should contain information about the holiday in a different time period. They should start with the Romans with characters explaining what they are celebrating, and be sure to illustrate the pamphlet. One section should include information from the time when the holiday was changed. The last section should explain our current Valentine's Day traditions.

President's Day

BOOKTALK

St. George, Judith; illustrated by David Small. *So You Want to Be President?* New York: Philomel, 2000. IL 3–6, RL 4.2 (Nonfiction)

Have you ever thought that some day it might be cool to be the president of the United States? Wonder what it would be like? Then this is the book for you. Unlike many boring books about the presidency, this book is filled with cool information about things like presidential hobbies, sports, and interests. Did you know that the president has his own bowling alley, swimming pool, and movie theater right in the White House? There are advantages to being the president. But there are disadvantages, too: He has to dress up and be nice to people! Well, you'll find out. Be sure to check out *So You Want to Be President*—even if you don't!

LEARNING EXTENSION IDEAS

1. Have students brainstorm the qualities that make a president. Have them discuss which president illustrates each quality or characteristic. Have the class reach a consensus on a list of characteristics needed to be a good president. Then have each student write a paragraph about why he or she would or would not be a good president.

2. Have the students create trading cards for the presidents. One side should have a picture of the president. This can be printed from the Internet, photocopied from a book, or drawn by the student. The president's name and dates of service should also be on that side. The other side can include information about the president, presented in a bulleted list. In addition to the using this book, students can find information on the Internet and in the library. Two good Web sites are Internet Public Library, at http://www.ipl.org/ref /POTUS and Lists of Presidents, at http://www.fujisan.demon.co .uk/USPresidents/preslist.htm.

Independence Day

BOOKTALK

Freedman, Russell. *Give Me Liberty! The Story of the Declaration of Independence.* New York: Holiday House, 2000. IL 5–8, RL 6.1 (Nonfiction)

Give me liberty or give me death! Do you know who said that? These were the words that Patrick Henry cried out in March 1775. The American Colonies were displeased with the way Great Britain was ruling them. There was a movement afoot to dissolve the union with Great Britain and create a united independent country. Revolution was in the air. Shortly thereafter a group of determined men affixed their signatures on the Declaration of Independence. Today, we celebrate July 4 as a national holiday. The day is filled with parades, barbecues, flag waving, and fireworks. Do you know why? To find out what this day is really all about, read this fascinating story about the writing of The Declaration of Independence. And find out what it means for you today.

LEARNING EXTENSION IDEAS

1. Have students research and investigate the origins of our holiday traditions. Ask them: Why do we celebrate Independence Day the way we do? Do other countries celebrate their independence? Why or why not?

2. Have students write a personal Declaration of Independence, in the style in which The Declaration of Independence is written. What do they think are their "rights" as opposed to privileges? Then have them work together to write a students' Declaration of Independence.

Halloween

BOOKTALK

Irving, Washington. *The Legend of Sleepy Hollow.* New York: Books of Wonder, 1990. IL 5–8, RL 8.9

Have you heard of the headless horseman? You know, the ghost that comes out each Halloween, searching for his head? Maybe you have a spare head that he can have? *The Legend of Sleepy Hollow* takes place in the late eighteenth century. Ichabod Crane has just moved from Connecticut to a town in upstate New York in search of a position as a schoolteacher. Unable to find regular work, he ends up going from house to house as a tutor. One of his students is the beautiful Katrina Van Tassel, the daughter of one of the town's wealthiest citizens. Ichabod becomes infatuated with Katrina. He is determined to marry her. Unfortunately, Katrina already has a boyfriend, Abraham "Brom Bones" Brut. Brom Bones tells Ichabod about the terrifying ghost who haunts the woods in search of a head. Now it's Halloween. Ichabod must travel through the woods. It's getting dark, and there are strange rustlings all around.

LEARNING EXTENSION IDEAS

1. This book was written in the 1800s. The language may not be familiar to today's teens. Students should come up with a list of unfamiliar words and look up the definitions. Have students create crossword puzzles using the words and definitions. Crossword puzzles can be created using the Web site at http://www.puzzlemaker.com.

2. To explore how words change over time, have students select a passage from the book. Have them rewrite the passage using current slang. Ask them: Does that make the story more powerful or less?

3. The ending of this tale is not definitive. Have students write an ending to the story, answering the following questions: Who is the Headless Horseman? What happens to Ichabod? Do you think Ichabod really became a lawyer?

Thanksgiving

BOOKTALK

Greenwood, Barbara; illustrated by Heather Collins. *A Pioneer Thanksgiving: A Story of Harvest Celebrations in 1841.* Buffalo, N.Y.: Kids Can Press, 1999. IL 3–6, RL 4.6

Join a pioneer family to celebrate Thanksgiving the old way. The Robertson family lives in the backwoods in the year 1841. The children gather cranberries for sauce and chestnuts for stuffing. Watch as they make bread and listen to Mr. Burkholder's stories. This book is filled with holiday traditions from long ago. You can actually make the crafts and cook the meals that are described because there are recipes and instructions. Celebrate holiday traditions from long ago in *A Pioneer Thanksgiving.*

LEARNING EXTENSION IDEAS

1. This book is filled with great ideas to use in the classroom to celebrate the Thanksgiving season. Have students choose one of the crafts in the book to share with the class.

2. Have students share their family Thanksgiving traditions. Not everyone celebrates with turkey and family get-togethers. Find out what others may do to celebrate.

Ramadan

BOOKTALK

Matthews, Mary. *Magid Fasts for Ramadan.* New York: Clarion Books, 1996. IL 3–6, RL 3.5

Eight-year-old Magid is determined to celebrate Ramadan. The young boy wants to fast from sunrise and sunset, as is the custom of Egyptian Muslims. Unfortunately, only boys 12 years old or over can participate in the fast. Magid convinces his mother to let him at least skip breakfast. But Magid is determined to join the men around him in the religious fast honoring Allah.

He secretly feeds his lunch to the geese and tries to participate in the fasting days. What will happen to Magid? Will he come to understand the true meaning of the fast?

LEARNING EXTENSION IDEAS

1. Have students research information about Ramadan. Ask them: What are the Five Pillars of Islam? When is Ramadan celebrated? What is the significance of the fast of Ramadan?

2. Ask students: Where is Ramadan celebrated? Students should create a map that indicates countries where very large populations practice Islam.

Hanukkah

BOOKTALK

Goldin, Barbara Diamond. *While the Candles Burn: Eight Stories for Hanukkah.* New York: Viking, 1996. IL 5–8, RL 6.0 (Nonfiction)

How much do you know about the Jewish festival of Hanukkah? This book offers eight stories on Hanukkah's themes. Learn about the eight nights of Hanukkah. What is the meaning of each night? The tales are based in the spiritual teachings of Judaism. The author goes beyond just telling the meaning of the celebration. She also tells how it fits into modern, contemporary life. What does a soccer game or a forgotten lunch have to do with Hanukkah? Well, you'll just have to pick up a copy of this book to find out.

LEARNING EXTENSION IDEAS

1. Ask students: Why is Hanukkah celebrated by Jewish people?

2. Have students list some of the symbols associated with the holiday and explain what the symbols represent?

Christmas

BOOKTALK

Avi. *The Christmas Rat.* New York: Atheneum Books for Young Readers, 2000. IL 3–6, RL 4.3

The week of Christmas vacation looms long for Eric Andrick. His best friend has gone to Florida, and his other friend is home sick. His parents are working all week. Eric faces a long week alone in his apartment all day long. On Monday, his mother tells him the exterminator is coming and to let him in. It's pretty unusual for the exterminator to come in the winter, but the building superintendent said it's routine. When the guy shows up, Eric lets him in to do his thing. The man, Anje Gabrail, is odd—and a little scary. He talks about how much he loves to kill things. Anje says since he can't kill people, vermin is the next best thing. People pay him to do it and are happy when he succeeds. He especially likes to kill rats! Anje inducts Eric into his rat-killing squad. He tells Eric to call anytime, day or night, if he spots a rat. As luck would have it, Eric goes to the basement to get the family's Christmas decorations, and there's a rat chewing the Christmas angel that they put on the top of the tree. When he tells Anje, they make it their quest to kill the rat by Christmas. They call it their Christmas rat. As the days go by, Eric begins to have doubts. He wonders if what they are trying to do is right. Why should they kill the rat? Do rats really all need to be exterminated?

LEARNING EXTENSION IDEAS

1. Ask students: What do you think of Anje? Do you think he is a real exterminator—or something else? Remember, no one else in the building has ever seen him! Draw a picture of Anje.

2. Anje's business card includes his phone number. It turns out that it is in code. The author challenges us to figure it out. Can the class do it?

BOOKTALK

Robinson, Barbara. *The Best Christmas Pageant Ever.* New York: HarperTrophy, 1988. IL 3–6, RL 5.1

Have you ever been involved with a Christmas pageant? Maybe you played a shepherd or an angel or even a character with lines. So you know that you need to learn your lines, attend rehearsals, and pay attention to the director. Well, not in this book. At first, it seemed as if the church pageant would go off as usual. But then the Herdman children decide to try out for the play. They have their reasons for wanting to be in the play. The Herdman children are just not like the other kids. In fact, they are some of the worst kids you can imagine. They lie, smoke cigars, and talk dirty. Why, they even set fire to Fred Shoemaker's old broken-down toolhouse. Now it looks like the Herdmans might totally ruin the pageant. Is there any hope?

LEARNING EXTENSION IDEAS

1. Have students research Christmas/Hanukkah or other holiday traditions from their cultural or religious backgrounds. Are the traditions that are practiced in the countries their ancestors came from still practiced in their households?

2. Have students select one of their traditions to demonstrate to the class. This can be done with a poster, a ceremony, a computer presentation, food preparation, and so forth. Students should be able to explain the origin of each tradition.

Kwanzaa

BOOKTALK

Karenga, Maulana. *Kwanzaa: A Celebration of Family, Community, and Culture.* Los Angeles: University of Saknore Press, 1998. IL YA (Nonfiction)

Have you heard of the celebration of Kwanzaa? Do you know what it is? How it started? What it celebrates? Maulana Karenga created this holiday in 1965. Dr. Karenga based the holiday on his African roots. Kwanzaa is an African-American and Pan-African holiday that celebrates family, community, and culture. It is celebrated from December 26 through January 1. Here, Dr. Karenga explains the background of the holiday. We also learn about the Seven Principles of Kwanzaa and the meaning of the symbols used. We learn how to celebrate the holiday and find out what the holiday is all about.

LEARNING EXTENSION IDEAS

1. The name Kwanzaa comes from the Swahili phrase meaning "first fruits." Ask students: How does this phrase reflect the holiday? What are the five fundamental activities of "first fruit" celebrations?

2. "First fruits" celebrations date back as far as Ancient Egypt and Nubia. Have students research other "first fruits" celebrations and show how they are incorporated into the modern day Kwanzaa celebration.

Suggested Further Reading

Cohen, Barbara. *Molly's Pilgrim.* New York: Lothrop, Lee & Shepard Books, 1998. IL 3–6, RL 2.8

Told to make a Pilgrim doll for the Thanksgiving display at school, Molly is embarrassed when her mother tries to help her out by creating a doll dressed as she herself was dressed before leaving Russia to seek religious freedom.

Dickens, Charles. *A Christmas Carol.* New York: Knopf/ Random House, ©1994. IL 5–8, RL 8.9

A miser learns the true meaning of Christmas when three ghostly visitors review his past and foretell his future.

Giblin, James. *Fireworks, Picnics, and Flags.* New York: Clarion Books, ©1983. IL 3–6, RL 7.2

Traces the social history behind America's celebration of Independence Day and explains the background of such national symbols as the flag, the bald eagle, the Liberty Bell, and Uncle Sam.

Henry, O. *The Gift of the Magi.* Nashville, Tenn.: Ideal Children's Books, ©1994. IL 5–8, RL 3.5

A simplified version of the well-known tale in which a husband and wife sacrifice treasured possessions so that they may buy each other Christmas presents.

Junior Worldmark Encyclopedia of World Holidays. Detroit: UXL, ©2000. IL 5–8, RL 7.2

Provides general overviews of 11 holidays celebrated in 30 countries and contains details on how each holiday is observed in one or more countries, discussing the history, stories, customs, clothing or costumes, food, arts and games, symbols, and music associated with each celebration.

Nathan, Joan. *The Children's Jewish Holiday Kitchen: 70 Ways to Have Fun with Your Kids and Make Your Family's Celebrations Special.* New York: Schocken Books; distributed by Pantheon Books, ©1995. IL 5–8, RL 7.3

Explains basic cooking techniques and includes easy-to-follow recipes for a variety of traditional dishes for holidays throughout the year; also includes instructions for related craft projects.

Salamon, Julie. *The Christmas Tree.* New York: Random House, ©1996. IL 5–8, RL 5.2

At Christmas time, a nun agrees to donate to Rockefeller Center a fir tree that has been her best friend since the time she arrived at her convent as a young orphan.

Sorensen, Lynda. *Memorial Day.* Vero Beach, Fla.: Rourke Press, ©1994. IL 3–6, RL 4.4

Discusses the Memorial Day holiday, including how it began, how it is celebrated, and the organizations that help continue the tradition.

Thacker, Nola. *Till's Christmas.* New York: Scholastic, ©1991. IL 5–8, RL 6.9

Eleven-year-old Till, a modern-day Scrooge, thinks her family's Christmas customs are hokey—until she catches the Christmas spirit.

Tolan, Stephanie S. *Save Halloween!* New York: Beech Tree, 1997. IL 5–8, RL 5.5

Eleven-year-old Johnna, who is deeply involved in the sixth-grade Halloween pageant although her family views it as a celebration of an un-Christian holiday, decides that she must follow her own beliefs.

Author/Title Index

Subject Index

ABOUT THE AUTHOR

Nancy J. Keane is a school librarian in Concord, New Hampshire. She has been a lover of children's literature all her life. In addition to her work in the school, Nancy also hosts a radio show on WKXL radio in Concord. *Kids Book Beat* is a monthly show that features children from the area booktalking about their favorite books. Nancy has also authored a children's fiction book and several books on booktalking.

She is the author of an award-winning Web site, *BOOKTALKS— QUICK AND SIMPLE* (http://www.nancykeane.com/booktalks). In addition, she has set up a listserv to bring together people who want to discuss book-talking and share booktalks: booktalkers@yahoogroups.com is an open list that welcomes new members.

Nancy is an adjunct faculty member at New Hampshire Technical College, Connected University, and teaches workshops for the University of New Hampshire.

She lives in Concord, New Hampshire, with her children, Aureta and Alex. They share their home with their dog and four cats.